What is Qualitative Research?

BW

'What is?' Research Methods series

Edited by Graham Crow, University of Southampton

ISSN: 2048–6812

The 'What is?' series provides authoritative introductions to a range of research methods which are at the forefront of developments in the social sciences. Each volume sets out the key elements of the particular method and features examples of its application, drawing on a consistent structure across the whole series. Written in an accessible style by leading experts in the field, this series is an innovative pedagogical and research resource.

What is Online Research?
Using the Internet for Social Science Research
Tristram Hooley, Jane Wellens and John Marriott
ISBN (HB): 9781780933344
ISBN (PB): 9781849665247
ISBN (ebook): 9781849665551

What is Social Network Analysis?
John Scott
ISBN (HB): 9781780938486
ISBN (PB): 9781849668170
ISBN (ebook): 9781849668194

What is Qualitative Research?
Martyn Hammersley
ISBN (HB): 9781780933351
ISBN (PB): 9781849666060
ISBN (ebook): 9781849666091

What are Qualitative Research Ethics?
Rose Wiles
ISBN (HB): 9781780938509
ISBN (PB): 9781849666527
ISBN (ebook): 9781849666541

What is Discourse Analysis?
Stephanie Taylor
ISBN (HB): 9781780938493
ISBN (PB): 9781849669030
ISBN (ebook): 9781849669061

What are Community Studies?
Graham Crow
ISBN (HB): 9781780933337
ISBN (PB): 9781849665957
ISBN (ebook): 9781849665988

Forthcoming books:

What is Qualitative Interviewing?
Rosalind Edwards and Janet Holland
ISBN (HB): 9781780938523
ISBN (PB): 9781849668095
ISBN (ebook): 9781849668019

What is Narrative Research?
Molly Andrews, Mark Davis, Cigdem Esin, Lar-Christer Hyden, Margareta Hyden, Corinne Squire and Barbara Harrison
ISBN (HB): 9781849669702
ISBN (PB): 9781849669733
ISBN (ebook): 9781849669702

What is Inclusive Research?
Melanie Nind
ISBN (HB): 9781780938516
ISBN (PB): 9781849668118
ISBN (ebook): 9781849668125

What is qualitative research?

Martyn Hammersley

BLOOMSBURY
NEW DELHI • LONDON • OXFORD • NEW YORK • SYDNEY

BLOOMSBURY INDIA
Bloomsbury Publishing India Pvt. Ltd
Second Floor, LSC Building No. 4, DDA Complex, Pocket C–6&7,
Vasant Kunj, New Delhi 110070

BLOOMSBURY, BLOOMSBURY ACADEMIC INDIA and the Diana logo are
trademarks of Bloomsbury Publishing Plc

First published in India 2023
First published in 2013
Reprinted 2013

This edition published with permission from Bloomsbury Publishing Plc,
50 Bedford Square, London, WC1B3DP, UK

British Library Cataloguing-in-Publication Data
A catalogue record for this book is available from the British Library

Library of Congress Cataloging-in-Publication Data
A catalog record for this book is available from the Library of Congress

ISBN: 978-93-54358-25-8

Printed and bound in India by Replika Press Pvt. Ltd.

To find out more about our authors and books
visit www.bloomsbury.com and sign up for our newsletters

Contents

Series foreword

The idea behind this series is a simple one: to provide concise and accessible overviews of a range of frequently-used research methods and of current issues in research methodology. Books in the series have been written by experts in their fields with a brief to write about their subject for a broad audience who are assumed to be interested but not necessarily to have any prior knowledge. The series is a natural development of presentations made in the 'What is?' strand at Economic and Social Research Council Research Methods Festivals which have proved popular both at the Festivals themselves and subsequently as a resource on the website of the ESRC National Centre for Research Methods.

Methodological innovation is the order of the day, and the 'What is?' format allows researchers who are new to a field to gain an insight into its key features, while also providing a useful update on recent developments for people who have had some prior acquaintance with it. All readers should find it helpful to be taken through the discussion of key terms, the history of how the method or methodological issue has developed, and the assessment of the strengths and possible weaknesses of the approach through analysis of illustrative examples.

The history of how qualitative methods have developed can seem particularly complicated, but the account offered here provides an accessible analysis of why this is the case and an explanation of why someone looking for a simple answer to the question 'what is qualitative research?' upon which everyone can agree is bound to be disappointed. In a field full of long-standing disputes, an account that locates the bases of the competing perspectives serves a valuable purpose in helping readers to get their bearings. The author's development in this context of his own distinctive argument about what is and what is not social science adds to the benefits readers can expect to derive.

The books cannot provide information about their subject matter down to a fine level of detail, but they will equip readers with a powerful sense of reasons why it deserves to be taken seriously and, it is hoped, with the enthusiasm to put that knowledge into practice.

Graham Crow
Series editor

Preface

Qualitative research, in a wide variety of forms, has become very influential across many fields of social science over the past fifty years. It originally emerged out of resistance to the previously common assumption that quantitative measurement, experimental method, and/or statistical analysis are essential if the knowledge produced by social science is not to be 'meagre' and 'unsatisfactory' (Thomson 1889: 73–4; see Merton *et al.* 1984). However, while qualitative researchers are agreed in their opposition to this definition of scientific research, or at least its application to social inquiry, beyond this there is little general consensus amongst them today. There are sharp disagreements about how research should be pursued, the epistemological and ontological assumptions on which it ought to rely, and even about its purpose or function. Given this, we might ask: What exactly does the term 'qualitative research' now mean? And also: Is it useful to think of it, any longer, as referring to a distinctive, coherent, and worthwhile approach? These are the questions around which this book is organized.

Many books, very different in character, could be, and indeed have been, written on this topic, each reflecting, to some extent, the experience and preferences of the author, these necessarily being the product of a particular social, cultural, and intellectual path. However, my main aim here has not been to present my own views about qualitative research, but rather to outline its character and variety, and to explore some of the disputes that surround and shape it, and their implications.

I am very grateful to several people for their comments on an earlier draft of the book: Graham Crow, the editor of the series in which it appears, Stephanie Taylor, Anna Traianou, and two colleagues who served as readers for the publisher. I am sure that it has been improved as a result, even though I know that I have failed to address adequately all of the issues they raised.

1 Defining qualitative research

The question 'What is qualitative research?' demands a definition of some sort: an account of what the phrase means. There is, of course, a very large methodological literature dealing with qualitative inquiry, and many definitions have been provided. Here are a couple of examples:

> Qualitative research is a research strategy that usually emphasizes words rather than quantification in the collection and analysis of data. (Bryman 2008a: 366)

> Qualitative research is an umbrella term for an array of attitudes towards and strategies for conducting inquiry that are aimed at discovering how human beings understand, experience, interpret, and produce the social world. (Sandelowski 2004: 893)

While both these definitions are certainly broadly accurate – and neither, of course, exhausts what these authors say about qualitative research – they pick out very different defining features. Other definitions offer additional features. For example, in a chapter entitled 'What is Qualitative Research?', Pertti Alasuutari (1995: 7) identifies its central feature as a particular kind of analysis: whereas quantitative work seeks to explain outcomes by examining the frequency with which they are empirically associated with possible causes, qualitative analysis employs a type of reasoning that is analogous to riddle-solving. He explains this as follows:

> Any single hint or clue could apply to several things, but the more hints there are to the riddle, the smaller the number of possible solutions. Yet each hint or piece of information is of its own kind and equally important; in unriddling – or qualitative analysis – [...] [e]very hint is supposed to fit in with the picture offered as the solution.

As these three definitions make clear, what are taken as the defining criteria of qualitative research can vary considerably. This perhaps tells us that it is not a simple phenomenon, not one that is easily characterized.

Ideally, in trying to understand what qualitative research is we are looking for a set of features that are shared by all examples of it, and that are *not* found together in other kinds of research. None of the definitions we have discussed is successful in these terms. While that provided by Alan Bryman captures something important, the main feature it identifies is, in effect, a negative one – the absence of quantification. After all, the presence of words in data collection and analysis is not distinctive to qualitative research: words are central to questionnaires, a common source of quantitative data; and there are generally more words than numbers in the analysis sections of quantitative research reports.[1]

Nor does Margarete Sandelowski's definition fit these requirements. Interpreted at face value, 'discovering how human beings understand, experience, interpret, and produce the social world' is the goal of a great deal, if not all, of social inquiry, not just that normally listed under the heading of 'qualitative'. For example, much survey research has been concerned with documenting differences in attitude with a view to explaining people's behaviour. Of course, it may be that what she intends by words like 'understand', 'experience' and 'interpret' is distinctive, but at face value it is not clear what marks out qualitative research here.

Finally, while Alasuutari's use of the riddle-solving metaphor is instructive, I doubt that the mode of reasoning he identifies is limited to qualitative work. Indeed, Susan Haack (2009) has argued that natural science, and all forms of inquiry, can best be understood as operating in a manner similar to solving a cross-word puzzle, a task that involves relating ideas about what the solution to a clue might be (empirical data) to hints from the letters supplied by answers to other clues (existing knowledge) – a process that parallels very closely what is involved in riddle-solving, as described by Alasuutari.

As I have already indicated, the problems with these definitions do not reflect a failure on the part of the authors concerned. Rather, they reveal that the task of providing an account of the distinctive features of qualitative research is far from straightforward. Indeed, trying to produce a list of

1 Campbell (1975) famously made the point that quantitative research is always founded on acts of 'qualitative knowing'.

features that *all* of what might be identified as qualitative inquiry shares, and that are *exclusive to it*, is almost certainly a hopeless venture. Later we will see why this is.

Nevertheless, we can, perhaps, produce a list of features that, in combination, frequently characterize what would be referred to as qualitative research. A number of strategies could be used. One is to appeal to the root terms from which the phrase has been historically derived. This *etymological* method is illustrated by Fred Erickson's (2011: 43) definition: 'From Latin, *qualitas* refers to a primary focus on qualities, the features, of entities – to distinctions in kind – while the contrasting term *quantitas* refers to a primary focus on differences in amount.' Appeals to etymology can sometimes be illuminating – in this case what it produces is similar to definitions produced in others ways, for example that of Bryman.

Another strategy would be to look at examples and to try to identify features that are frequently present. Box 1.1 provides summaries of a small selection of studies that would probably be regarded as clear instances of qualitative inquiry.

Box 1.1 Exemplars of qualitative research

Morton on 'becoming tongan'

Having visited Tonga as a teenager, lived in Tongan households in Australia, and later married a Tongan, the anthropologist Helen Morton (1996) carried out eight months' ethnographic fieldwork living in a village there, along with her young son. She observed what went on and talked to people in the village, recording her data in the form of fieldnotes; though she also used a questionnaire distributed to secondary school students. Her aim was to study the experience of childhood in that society – what it means to become Tongan – seeking as part of this to understand the rather harsh treatment to which Tongan children are often subjected.

Rai on 'positive loitering'

This was a 'critical' ethnographic study of a 'community policing' practice introduced by the Chicago Alternative Policing Strategy (CAPS) as a way for community members to combat 'gang presence, public drinking, criminal behavior, and drug activity' (Rai 2011: 66). The author examines how 'positive loitering' was used in a 'gentrifying

Chicago neighborhood' to try to eradicate an informal street labour market. It involved 'passive-aggressive flash mob actions where people simply show up and hangout in the spaces where the laborers gather' (Rai 2011: 67). She observed monthly CAPS meetings, and interventions on the street, and interviewed 'positive loiterers', some of the people seeking work, and the organizer of the market. She argues that positive loitering highlights how 'democratic and neoliberal rhetoric can dovetail in local practices that obscure systemic inequality [...]; and expose the ambivalence of civic participation' (Rai 2011: 68).

Wacquant on boxing

Loïc Wacquant, a French sociologist working in the United States, became an apprentice boxer 'by default and by accident' as part of a study of 'the everyday reality of the black American ghetto' (Wacquant 2004: viii). He emphasizes the value of 'theoretically armed' participant observation, drawing on the work of the French sociologist Pierre Bourdieu. His aim was 'to plumb the inner depths' of what it means to be a boxer, so as to capture and represent 'the taste and the ache' of this profession, as pursued in this community (Wacquant 2004: vii). In sociological terms, the task was to document the dispositions and skills involved, and how they are developed and deployed. His data were fieldnotes written up each evening after being in the gym (Wacquant 2004: ix–x).

Bogdan on the autobiography of Jane Fry

In the early 1970s, Robert Bogdan (1974) carried out a series of life history interviews, several times a week over a period of three months, with 'Jane Fry' (pseudonym), a transsexual born as a biological male who believed that she was a woman. He transcribed and edited around a hundred hours of audio-recorded material with a view to producing a sociological life history that conveyed her experience and perspective on life. Her 'autobiography' – an account in her own words, albeit composed from what she said in interviews – forms the central part of the book. In addition, Bogdan provides a commentary, drawing on medical records, that juxtaposes her perspective with those of the professionals who had been in contact with her at various times.

MacLure and Walker on parents' evenings in UK secondary schools

This is a study of the discursive practices displayed in 184 meetings (typically lasting around five minutes each) between teachers and parents in five UK secondary schools (MacLure and Walker 2000). The audio-recordings were made by two teachers and two parents, without the presence of the researchers; though the latter had observed a parents' evening in each school. Follow-up interviews were carried out with a small number of parents, teachers, and students. The authors examine the typical structure of these meetings in sociolinguistic terms. In particular, they document the 'interactional absence' of students even when they were physically present, the strong similarity in the pattern of the interaction despite considerable variation in the characteristics of the parties involved, and the dominant (though occasionally contested) role played by teachers.

Wetherell and Edley on masculinity

This research was based on thirty audio-recorded interviews with groups of British men (totaling 61) from diverse occupational backgrounds, varying in age from 20 to 64 (Wetherell and Edley 1999). A typical discussion group consisted of the interviewer (Nigel Edley) and two volunteers, although a few sessions involved three and others just one. In some interviews photographs of possible role models were used to stimulate conversation. On the basis of detailed discourse analysis of this material, the authors challenge the theoretical concept of 'hegemonic masculinity', examining specific practices by which men construct themselves as masculine. The authors state that 'We chose discourse as a site for investigating men's identities because we are persuaded of the central role discursive practices play in the constitution of subjectivity' (Wetherell and Edley 1999: 337).

Wright and Decker on armed robbers

Active armed robbers in St Louis, Missouri were contacted via a specially recruited and paid fieldworker who was an ex-criminal known to local criminals (Wright and Decker 1997). The researchers met their informants on the streets, and carried out semi-structured interviews asking about robberies in which the informants had been involved. They sometimes took the informant to the scene of a robbery to test his account; and also compared accounts provided by co-offenders. On the basis of these data, they drew conclusions about the role of motivational factors, situational features, and environmental cues in generating armed robberies.

Mitchell on survivalists

Survivalists are people who 'anticipate various kinds of imminent cataclysm – economic collapse, race war, nuclear attack, and so forth – and take steps to ensure their own postdisaster welfare' (Mitchell 1991: 97). They 'often eschew telephones, launder their mail through letter exchanges, use nicknames and aliases, and carefully conceal their addresses from strangers' (Mitchell 1991: 100). In order to document survivalist beliefs and practices Mitchell carried out participant observation, covert and overt, and interviews, and began to edit a group newsletter, with the result that he became 'the recipient of a steady stream of members' written opinions and perceptions' (Mitchell 1991: 100). This role then allowed him to use tape recorders and cameras at group meetings. In his book *Dancing at Armageddon* he provides a picture of the 'world' of survivalists and how it reflects and responds to salient features of modern industrial civilization (Mitchell 2001).

Frake on 'how to ask for a drink in Subanum'

In a classic study of an ethnic group who were farmers occupying part of the mountainous interior of an island in the Philippines, the author provides a detailed description of their drinking practices (Frake 1964a). This covers the types of drink available within the culture and focuses on how one of these, what he refers to as a type of beer, is drunk at religious festivities that serve important socio-political functions. His aim was to describe in detail what someone must know in order to be a competent member of this culture (Frake 1964b: 112). The information was obtained through observation but also by highly structured interviews designed to elicit the terminological distinctions – about types of drink and the activities surrounding them – employed by the Subanum.

Oliver and O'Reilly on lifestyle migration from Britain to Spain

This study involved a re-analysis of data, derived from observation and interviews, collected by the two authors in earlier, separate projects that had each led to a published account. The aim was to use secondary analysis to explore the continued relevance of social class in light of arguments about its declining influence in Western societies. Oliver and O'Reilly (2010: 49) argue that 'despite attempts to rewrite their own history and to mould a different life trajectory through geographical mobility' migrants reproduced class distinctions in and through their attitudes to other migrants and to tourists. Bourdieu's theoretical approach was employed here to explore the limited possibilities for reconstructing institutionalized dispositions in this field.

Olson *et al.* on suicide notes

This is a study in the sociology of health concerned with motivations for suicide (Olson *et al.* 2011). It offers a cross-cultural analysis of suicide notes written by Native Americans, Hispanics, and Anglos in New Mexico. Official records were used to identify those suicides where a suicide note was available. For ethical reasons the researchers did not contact family members to obtain additional information. The suicide notes ranged in length from several words to several pages, and took various forms, including a message on the back of a grocery bag. Five categories emerged describing motivation: feelings of alienation, of failure or inadequacy, being psychologically overwhelmed, the wish to leave problems behind, and a desire for reunification with another in an afterlife. It was concluded that the ethnic differences in patterns of response across these categories were surprisingly small.

Levitas on political rhetoric

This study examined official documents relating to social inclusion produced in the early years of the New Labour government in the United Kingdom. The author identifies three different discourses in these documents, and studies the relationships amongst them: a redistributive discourse (acronym, RED) with a primary focus on poverty and inequality; a moral underclass discourse (MUD) which concentrated on what is portrayed as the delinquent behaviour of those excluded; and a social integrationist discourse (SID) that emphasized the capacity of paid employment to facilitate people's 'reintegration' into society. The three discourses differ in what the excluded are portrayed as lacking: from the point of view of RED they have too little money, for SID the problem is that they have no work, while from the perspective of MUD they have no morals (Levitas 1998: 7). Levitas offers a critical analysis of how these discourses operated in New Labour policies.

Lewis on an online support group for irritable bowel syndrome

As part of work for a Masters thesis, Lewis (2006) became a participating member of an online support group for people with Irritable Bowel Syndrome (IBS), analyzing postings on bulletin boards and discussions in chatrooms. He supplemented these naturally occurring on-line data with a 'qualitative questionnaire', in other words a questionnaire with open-ended questions, sent and returned by email to participants who had agreed to complete it. His research examined how people with this condition experience their illness and use online support groups to cope with it.

Kaplan on engaging in action research with disadvantaged students through participatory photography

At the behest of a local education authority, Kaplan (2008) worked over a nine-month period with disadvantaged students and their teachers in several schools in the northwest of England. The aim was to facilitate students using photography to explore, and share, their perspectives on, and to improve their experiences of, education. Students were given a workshop on '"reading"/ interpreting photographs' and issues about ethics and consent, and were instructed in basic photographic technique. Subsequently, the photographs were discussed by the group and some of these selected and captioned for a powerpoint presentation. In one school, some of the photographs generated considerable conflict, and Kaplan reports that he was left with a sense that the school's senior management 'was unwilling or unable' to acknowledge the value of students' perspectives which challenged existing structures of teaching and learning (Kaplan 2008: 188).

The differences among the studies described in Box 1.1 are probably more striking than any commonalities, not just in terms of substantive focus but also in the methods employed. Some of them involve forms of participant observation – researchers going to particular social settings, observing and perhaps also taking on a participant role. Others rely entirely on interviews or on documentary evidence, of varying kinds. Also, some of the studies were concerned with portraying an aspect of the lives of the people concerned while others focus on analyzing forms of language-use or on explicating the categories characteristic of a particular culture.

So, the label 'qualitative research' covers a heterogeneous field. Moreover, we cannot conclude that any feature shared by two or more of the studies listed is relevant to defining 'qualitative research'. This is true, for example, of the fact that a couple of them used the work of Pierre Bourdieu: while his ideas are currently very influential in some quarters, qualitative inquiry draws on a very wide range of theoretical perspectives that differ quite sharply from one another.

The contrast with quantitative research

In trying to define 'qualitative research', it is important to remember that all questions, or all interpretations of them, involve an implicit or explicit 'frame'. In the case of 'what is?' questions, this relates to a typology of some sort: such questions are concerned with how one type of thing differs from something else. And the most obvious contrast in this case, indicated in some of the definitions I have already quoted, is: what is qualitative, *as opposed to quantitative*, research?

This is almost certainly the primary contrast that determines the meaning of the phrase 'qualitative research' in most contexts; though some have suggested that it is uninformative (Grahame 1999: 4; Silverman 2006: 33), and others that it is 'unadventurous' albeit necessary (Holliday 2002: 1). Yet, if we know the features of quantitative research, this can help us to some degree in identifying those of qualitative work, even if it does not tell us all that we might wish to know. Furthermore, this contrast is not just semantically primary but also reflects the historical development of qualitative inquiry: it emerged as a distinct kind of social science in competition with an already established tradition of quantitative method.

The label 'qualitative research' began to be widely used in the 1960s to identify deviation from the quantitative forms of research that were then dominant: experimental work in social psychology and some applied fields; survey research in sociology, political science, and other areas; the use of 'official statistics', notably in demography, economics, and health research; content analysis of media material; and structured observation, notably in education and criminology. It is not that qualitative data had not been used prior to this – indeed the development of specific quantitative methods was frequently motivated by a commitment to replace earlier types of non-quantitative data that were judged to be scientifically unsatisfactory. For example, questionnaires and tests were introduced as a more efficient and reliable method of gaining information about attitudes and values than the life history interviews that had previously been used (Stouffer 1930); predictive psychological tests were employed as an alternative to clinical interviews by psychologists (Meehl 1954); and structured forms of observation and interviewing were used as a substitute for more open-ended forms that failed to produce standardized data (see Platt 1996; Gobo 2011).

So, it was through opposition to previously used 'unscientific' methods that *quantitative work* came to be formulated as a distinct, labeled approach. And it increasingly came to be presented as generally being committed to:

1 *Hypothesis-testing*. An explicit research design is developed at the start of inquiry, which is aimed at testing some set of hypotheses. This is done through operationalising key variables: in other words, specifying the data that would be relevant to them, along with the instruments needed to produce these data, as well as the form of analysis to be employed.
2 *The use of numerical data*. Data take the form of specific counts of instances or of rankings/measurements of objects according to the degree to which they possess some feature. Measurement is often treated as superior to counting and ranking, and the ideal is to employ scales modeled on those used in natural science, such as in the measurement of temperature.
3 *Procedural objectivity*. Counting, ranking and measurement procedures must operate in ways that are 'objective', in the sense that they are standardized. This is designed to rule out bias caused

by the social and personal characteristics of the researcher, and to enable checks on the operation of such bias through replication.

4 *Generalization.* Samples may be studied with a view to generalizing to some larger population, and statistical techniques can be used to maximize the validity of the generalization and to assess the chances of serious error in the process.

5 *Identifying systematic patterns of association.* Statistical techniques are also used to describe the patterns to be found in the data, and perhaps also to test the likelihood that these could have been the product of random processes rather than of a systematic causal relationship.

6 *Controlling variables.* There is usually an attempt to control variables, physically via experimental method or 'statistically' through cross-case analysis of a large sample or population. This is designed to separate out what effects a 'treatment' or 'causal' variable has, on a particular type of outcome, from the systematic influence of other variables that might impact on it.

It was in the process of challenging the dominance of quantitative method, formulated in this way, that qualitative research itself came to be framed as a general style, approach, or 'paradigm' (see, for example, Filstead 1970). This challenge was based upon a number of arguments, including:

- the importance of studying what normally happens in the 'real' world, rather than what happens under experimental conditions;
- the need to *observe* what happens rather than to rely solely upon respondents' accounts in formal interviews or questionnaires;
- the need to allow people to speak in their own terms in interviews if we are to be able to undersand their distinctive perspectives;
- the danger that quantification results in the meaning of central concepts being lost;
- the concern that the kind of variable analysis employed by quantitative researchers ignores the complex, contingent and context-sensitive character of social life, and the extent to which actions and outcomes are produced by people *interpreting* situations in diverse ways, and acting on the basis of these interpretations, rather than passively responding to external causes.

In light of this contrast with quantitative social science, we can define 'qualitative research' along the following lines: *a form of social inquiry that tends to adopt a flexible and data-driven research design, to use relatively unstructured data, to emphasize the essential role of subjectivity in the research process, to study a small number of naturally occurring cases in detail, and to use verbal rather than statistical forms of analysis*. Each of these features requires further elaboration:

1. *A flexible, 'inductive', 'abductive', or data-driven orientation.* Qualitative researchers place more emphasis on generating and developing descriptions and explanations than upon testing pre-defined hypotheses. This means that a flexible research design is adopted, rather than one in which a detailed plan is laid out at the start of the research and then 'implemented'. This is also reflected at the stage of analyzing data, where the task is to generate categories rather than to place data into pre-determined ones. And the categories initially developed tend to be open-ended and flexible in character, so that each data item can be assigned to more than one of them. In other words, the categories do not form a mutually exclusive and exhaustive set, at least not at the start of the analytic process.
2. *Relatively unstructured kinds of data are used.* There is little pressure to engage in formal counting, ranking, or measurement. For example, in the case of observation, qualitative researchers watch carefully what is happening, and often try to write concrete descriptions in natural language that capture relevant aspects of what is observed and of how events unfold. Alternatively, or as a complement, audio- or video-recording is often used, with transcripts being produced on the basis of these. Similarly, in the case of interviews, qualitative research typically involves a relatively unstructured approach where the aim is to invite informants to talk at length about matters that are broadly relevant to the research, with the interviewer following up to encourage more elaboration, detail, or exemplification where necessary. Qualitative researchers may also use documentary data, such as official reports, newspapers and magazines, photographs, maps, diaries, and so on, without seeking to quantify their content in the manner of much content analysis. In recent years, there has been a growth in the use of visual data, seeking to counter the more common reliance upon text. There has also been increasing

use of material available electronically on the Internet. Qualitative researchers may also sometimes *elicit* documentary data, for example asking people to write diaries, produce drawings, take photographs, make videos, etc.

3 *Subjectivity*. There is acceptance, perhaps even celebration, of the fact that data, and inferences from them, are always shaped by the social and personal characteristics of the researcher. It is recognized that it is impossible to eliminate the effect of these, and indeed that they may facilitate insight as well as leading to error. It is sometimes argued that reflexivity – the provision of detailed information about the researcher and the research process – can enable readers to allow for any effects of the researcher's characteristics, or of how the research was carried out, that might obscure or threaten the validity of the analysis. In short, there is opposition to the idea that research should be a standardized and impersonal process – to any requirement that the personal be suppressed in the name of science. However, this does not necessarily imply opposition to the kind of concern with objectivity that requires researchers to assess and try to counter potential threats to the validity of their conclusions.

4 *The study of 'natural' settings*. Experimental research creates settings, for example in a laboratory, that are specifically designed to allow control over the treatment variable and to rule out confounding variables. And much non-experimental quantitative research relies upon questionnaires or formal interviews that are structured with the aim of standardizing the stimuli to which respondents are subjected, in order to render responses comparable. By contrast, most qualitative work investigates what goes on in the ordinary settings in which people live and work, and/or uses interviews that are designed to approximate to ordinary conversations in key respects.

5 *Small number of cases studied*. Survey research generally studies large samples in order to generalize across many cases, and/or to provide enough cases to employ comparative analysis so as to control variables. By contrast, qualitative inquiry often involves investigation of a small number of naturally occurring cases, perhaps just one. This stems from insistence on the need for in-depth examination of each case, in order to document complexity. Also involved is the argument that each feature of a case can only be understood within

the context of that case, because features will shape one another, rather than having pre-determined and fixed characters. There is opposition, then, to the tendency in quantitative research to rely upon data that have been extracted from their local contexts, for example questionnaire responses whose relationship to people's lives is uncertain. Furthermore, in-depth investigation of cases allows the checking of interpretations through comparison of data of different kinds, for example that from observation with that from interviews, or accounts from different informants. This is rarely possible in surveys.

6 *Verbal rather than statistical analysis of data.* The predominant mode of analysis is verbal description and interpretation, supported by illustrative or evocative examples. Such descriptions are sometimes seen as simultaneously fulfilling the functions of explanation, as for example with the notion of 'thick' or 'theoretical' description (see Geertz 1973; Hammersley 1992: ch.1). For instance, qualitative researchers are frequently concerned with discovering which factors tend to produce some outcome, or what the typical consequences of some event or type of action are, and they seek to do this through describing in detail changes in a small number of cases studied over time. The approach here is quite similar to that employed by historians, who produce narrative accounts of the events leading up to some outcome they are interested in explaining. Qualitative researchers may also compare one or more cases in order to try to assess which of several factors involved seem to play the crucial role in the sort of social processes being investigated.

By no means all of what is currently labeled qualitative research would share *all* of the features listed here, though much of it would display *most* of them. There may also be other features that some qualitative researchers would regard as essential. In addition, it is necessary to recognize that there are studies that *combine* quantitative and qualitative features, some being explicitly labeled 'mixed methods studies';[2] though usually one or other type of method plays the dominant role (Bryman 2007). Thus, while numerical data and analysis are employed in some qualitative studies, this is subordinated to the central use of relatively unstructured data and verbal forms of analysis.

2 On 'mixed methods', see Tashakkori and Teddlie (2010).

Methods or paradigms?

Having outlined the distinguishing features of quantitative and qualitative approaches to social research, we need to give some attention next to the question of the proper relationship between them. This has been a matter for debate and we can identify two sharply contrasting positions, though there is space for others between these. First, there are those who argue that qualitative and quantitative approaches are simply two sets of methods each of which is appropriate for tackling distinctive kinds of research question, and/or that can contribute complementary forms of evidence in addressing the same issue. Here the emphasis is on choosing the method, or combination of methods, that is 'fit for purpose'. At the other extreme are those who argue that qualitative and quantitative approaches involve divergent assumptions about the nature of the world, how (or even whether) we can gain knowledge of it, and the purpose of inquiry. On this basis, it is argued that they are incompatible, and perhaps even that only one of them is valid or legitimate; or, alternatively, they may be treated as each being valid in its own terms, so that researchers must make a choice between the two, perhaps as a matter of personal taste, analogous to how artists choose one style over another, or in the manner that people come to commit to a particular religion or to none (Schrodt 2006).

It is probably the case that most qualitative researchers today adopt the second of these two broad views: they regard quantitative and qualitative as incompatible approaches, with the latter judged superior.[3] At the same time, there have always been those who have adopted a position closer to the first view (see, for instance, Trow 1957 and Sieber 1973), and in recent times the idea of 'mixing' qualitative and quantitative methods has gained increasing influence (Bryman 2008b).

A different contrast

While the contrast with quantitative work is the most obvious frame within which to answer the question 'what is qualitative research?', others are possible, and will on occasion be relevant. So, for example, we could ask how qualitative inquiry differs from journalism, from other kinds

3 There are fields where this is not the case, notably political science where qualitative case study work has been promoted as an important *complement* to quantitative method (see Brady and Collier 2004; Mahoney and Goertz 2006).

of non-fiction writing, or even from imaginative literature. Thus, how does Tapper's (2006) anthropological study of Afghanistan differ from Seierstad's (2002) *The Bookseller of Kabul*, which is also primarily concerned with the nature of marriage and family life in that country? Similarly, how does Buford's (1991) journalistic account of his encounters with 'football thugs' relate to Armstrong's (1998) sociological account of soccer fans and the violence in which they are sometimes involved? As we shall see, the relationship between qualitative research and these other forms of writing has become increasingly central to the way in which some qualitative researchers think about the enterprise in which they are engaged.

In the past, qualitative researchers usually sought to draw a sharp distinction between their work and that of journalists and novelists, and some still do. Here, for example, is Armstrong's commentary on Buford's book:

> [this] supposedly factual account [...], translated into 40 languages, is a self-aggrandising journey amongst fans who obviously wondered why this 40-year-old American was in their midst. The author, in pursuit of fitting in with his subjects, admits to pushing two pensioners down a railway station staircase while abusing them, such was his supposed method acting. This confused man produced a poor book that was more fictional than a novel; Buford fortunately did not spend too much time with his hooligans, and the account is more about narcissistic contemplations than about the 'thugs' apparently representative of 'a country of little shits'. With this state of play the question could be raised as to what else there is that a reader needs to know on the subject? If they will bear with me I believe what follows is different, combining, as it does, first-hand accounts with a theoretical explanation. (Armstrong 1998: 19–20)

There are multiple accusations here: that Buford's account is not accurate, that this stems from the fact that he was not able to fit in with and be accepted by the soccer fans he was studying, (by ironic implication) that he did not spend long enough with them to gain the necessary understanding, that he had the wrong attitude ('self-aggrandizing', 'narcissistic') and was 'confused', and that he fails to provide 'a theoretical explanation'.[4]

---

4 It is also suggested that Buford's behaviour was unethical, but I will leave this on one side here. On ethical issues in qualitative research, see Hammersley and Traianou (2012).

Many qualitative researchers would also argue that a distinctive feature of their work is that it is based upon the systematic collection, recording, and analysis of data. However, non-fiction writers and even novelists often carry out background research in order to try to make their accounts accurate, or at least plausible. For example Seierstad spent several months living in Kabul, having previously served as a reporter elsewhere in Afghanistan covering the war. Furthermore, she notes that while she had to rely upon just three members of the family with whom she lived as her interpreters and major informants, she 'double-checked the various versions and asked the same questions of all three [...] who between them represented the large contrasts within the family' (Seierstad 2002: 5).[5] There is clearly at least some attention here to the reliability of her data and conclusions, even if these may not meet the requirements of social science. And while Buford's 'fieldwork' may have been inadequate from Armstrong's point of view, he spent a considerable amount of time with fans in many locations.

In fact, what Armstrong seems to object to most strongly is Buford's negative evaluations of soccer fans. It is a central feature of some qualitative research that an 'appreciative' (Matza 1969) stance is adopted towards the people being studied, especially when they are vilified or marginalised within the wider society. Sometimes this is seen as a matter of 'whose side are we on?', though in fact the article that famously raised this question (Becker 1967) does not argue for siding with the underdog. Rather, it insists on the need to avoid evaluations of the people, actions, institutions, etc being studied, and on the requirement to document the perspectives of all parties, while taking the validity of none of these at face value (Hammersley 2000: ch.3). Moreover, it should be said that, in fact, an appreciative stance is rarely adopted as a consistent policy by qualitative researchers today across all the types of people they study. Indeed Armstrong himself engages in evaluation, for example labelling some press coverage of football violence 'hysterical' (Armstrong 1998: 93), and criticizing football clubs for 'milking' fans for profit (Armstrong 1998: 130).

Another difference that may be held to distinguish qualitative research from journalism and imaginative literature concerns the form of writing

5 The bookseller whose family Seierstad studied subsequently read the book and mounted a prosecution of the author. See: http://www.guardian.co.uk/theguardian/2010/jul/31/bookseller-of-kabul-interview-asne-seierstad

employed. Thus, in her study of marriage and family in Afghanistan, Tapper adopts a fairly conventional social scientific mode of exposition, whereas Seierstad describes her writing as 'literary' (2004: 3), deploying a 'storytelling' style, and one that is addressed to a general readership rather than to a more specialized social science one. Much the same is true if we compare the books of Buford and Armstrong. The first author concentrates on telling a story about his various encounters with football fans, whereas Armstrong seeks systematically to locate the data from his participant observation within a broader picture of the social organization of soccer clubs, as well as changes in legislation and policing in the United Kingdom relating to football violence.

However, these are differences of degree, they do not represent a dichotomy, and there are factors working to blur any difference between social science and journalism in the mode of writing employed. One of these is that in recent years there has been pressure on social scientists to maximize the dissemination of their findings, alongside a growing commitment among some of them to 'public sociology' (Burawoy 2005) or 'civic sociology' (Wacquant 2009). An effect of this has been to encourage a move towards forms of reporting that are closer in character to those of journalists and non-fiction writers. Indeed, there have been studies by academic social scientists that have deployed a 'storytelling' mode of presentation that is quite similar to that of Seierstad and Buford. An example is Venkatesh's (2008) investigation of Chicago gangs, in which he begins by recounting how he set out from the campus of the University of Chicago to do research in the predominantly black and poor community of Woodlawn nearby, stumbling into a house that was controlled by one of the local drug gangs. Where some qualitative research studies begin with descriptive narrative of this kind, subsequently shifting to a more academic mode, or more generally intersperse narrative data with sociological analysis (see, for example, Duneier's *Slim's Table*, which is set in more or less the same community), Venkatesh's book continues throughout in the same narrative mode. Its subtitle, *A Rogue Sociologist Crosses the Line*, more or less sums up its content.

Another possible answer to the question of the distinctiveness of qualitative research in this context would, of course, be that it is scientific, whereas journalism and (even more obviously) novel-writing are not. But this raises the fraught question of what the term 'scientific' means in this context. Moreover, in recent years many qualitative researchers have become more uncertain about whether they are engaged in science, and what this entails. Indeed, some have rejected this aspiration, appealing instead to models from the humanities and the arts. As part of this, the parallels between the rhetorical styles employed in qualitative inquiry and those used by both non-fiction writers and novelists have been noted (Atkinson 1983 and 1990; Brown 1989). Furthermore, some qualitative researchers have turned to producing fictions, poetry, and drama as research reports (see Ellis and Bochner 1996; Richardson and St. Pierre 2005; Faulkner 2009). There has also been increasing interest in life history, biographical methods, and autoethnography, which in recent years have been taken in directions that have very close relations to literary forms of biography and autobiography (Plummer 2001; Bochner and Ellis 2002; Ellis 2004). A parallel development has been the move among some qualitative researchers to visual or multi-modal methods, in some cases deliberately blurring any distinction between their research and visual art forms.[6] In short, many qualitative researchers have either abandoned the model of science – explicitly or implicitly – or have sought to reinterpret it in much broader and more diverse terms (see Denzin and Lincoln 2011: 10).

By contrast with these developments in the qualitative tradition, quantitative researchers have generally remained unequivocally committed to the scientific model, relying upon relatively traditional interpretations of this. As a result, the shift in orientation among qualitative researchers just mentioned has not only made any difference harder to delineate between their work and non-fiction writing and journalism, and even imaginative literature or art, but has also increased the divergence between qualitative and quantitative approaches.

Summary

In this opening chapter I have outlined the diversity of qualitative research, and the difficulties this creates for producing a definition of it. However, I offered one that listed some common features of this kind of work by contrast with quantitative approaches – in terms of specific practices

6 For discussions of the development of 'visual methods', see Banks (2001), Emmison and Smith (2000), Pink (2007), and Rose (2007). On multi-modal methods, see Dicks (2006) and Pink (2009).

relating to research design and the collection and analysis of data. I also noted that while qualitative researchers have traditionally sought to draw a sharp distinction between their work and that of journalists and novelists, in recent decades some have stressed the similarities instead. As part of this, they have rejected or reinterpreted the model of science, thus increasing the differences between their approach and that of quantitative researchers. Of course, the key question is *why* do qualitative researchers tend to work in very different ways from quantitative researchers? One answer is that the two approaches have been shaped by divergent methodological philosophies. In the next chapter, we will explore some of these.

2 Methodological philosophies

This chapter will look at some of the philosophical ideas that have shaped the practice and development of qualitative research, and that continue to do so. These ideas, which relate to the nature of the social world (ontology), how knowledge of it is possible (epistemology), and to the purpose(s) of inquiry (which might be seen as an aspect of politics), can be complex and difficult. However, it is important to understand them.

Following on from the previous chapter, a useful starting point is to note that quantitative social science was, and in some respects continues to be, strongly influenced by one particular set of views about social research methodology, that have long been referred to as 'positivism'. Not surprisingly, perhaps, it is common to find qualitative researchers rejecting positivism and contrasting their own methodological ideas with it. Partly as a result, the meaning of this term has become largely negative – it is used almost exclusively as a means of dismissing other approaches. Thus, very few quantitative researchers today would actually call themselves positivists. The sense of the term 'positivism' has also become displaced, as a result of the fact that, in many substantive fields of social enquiry, a sequence of new qualitative approaches have appeared over time, each one denouncing their predecessors as positivist. Thus, an influential current interpretation applies the term to anyone who believes that there are truths that can be discovered about a common reality. An example is Plummer's (2001: x) self-critique of the 'thinly disguised positivistic concern with getting at the truth' that characterized the first edition of his own book on life history method (Plummer 1983).

Over the past few decades, then, there has been a diversification of qualitative research into competing versions, in large part due to the influence of methodological philosophies that stand opposed to positivism, and also as a result of the fact that these alternatives are in conflict with one another in important respects. In this chapter I will examine these philosophies under the broad headings of interpretivism, 'critical' research, and constructionism. However, we need to begin at the beginning, with positivism.[1]

Positivism

While the meaning of the word 'positivism' has become contextually variable, and almost always negative, we can nevertheless recover some important elements of its original sense, and these are worth remembering. The word was invented by the French philosopher Auguste Comte, and became the focus for a major intellectual – indeed a 'religious' – movement in France, and to some degree elsewhere (Pickering 1993; Charlton 1959; Wright 1986). For Comte, writing in the early nineteenth century, positivism was the modern scientific outlook that was in the process of replacing previously dominant supernatural ways of thinking about the world. And he developed a comprehensive view of the nature of science, and of the proper relationships among the various sciences. However, the most influential version of positivism for twentieth-century social science was a largely separate development in the 1920s and 1930s, what came to be called logical positivism or logical empiricism (Kolakowski 1972; Halfpenny 1982; Bryant 1985).[2] Perhaps the most important feature of positivism was that it took natural science, as developed in the West from the seventeenth century onwards, as the prime or only model for inquiry and knowledge. In this respect, it built upon central strands of eighteenth-century Enlightenment thought, although the sources of these can be traced back even earlier (see Olson 1993).

It is particularly significant that logical positivism generally took physics as its model for science. This had several consequences. One was that scientific knowledge was seen as general and abstract in form: consisting

1 There are no beginnings, of course, and it is important to remember that positivism itself developed out of a reaction against earlier ideas, notably those relating to natural law, see d'Entréves (1954), Sigmund (1971), Portis (1986), and Hammersley (1992). The labels for alternative philosophies I have used here, while in common currency, are by no means the only ones available. My discussion will, however, cover most of the influential philosophical ideas that have shaped qualitative research.

2 There were a variety of interpretations of natural science method in the nineteenth and twentieth centuries, and some of these specifically distanced themselves from positivism. They include, amongst many others, the 'critical rationalism' of Popper (see Albert 1985), and the 'critical realism' of Harré and Bhaskar (see Keat and Urry 1983; Sayer 2000).

of laws that capture relations operating across all times and places. The emphasis, then, was upon the need for research to abstract from the study of particular situations to produce such general knowledge. As a result, there was a tendency for historical change and cultural variation to be treated as mere appearances that can be explained only by an analysis of underlying, universal causal relations.[3] Newton's physics, with its identification of a small set of principles that govern the behaviour of all physical objects, whether in the heavens or on earth, was a key exemplar in this respect.

Another implication that followed from taking physics as a model was the requirement that all knowledge must be grounded in sense experience that is subjected to methodical control. This led many social scientists to insist on the need for rigorous measurement of phenomena, on the model of the measurement of physical attributes like length or temperature. Also emphasized was the need for experimental control of variables to test hypotheses. Furthermore, the notion of 'method' was taken to mean 'explicit procedures', with the implication that the conclusions reached would be the same whoever carried out the research, irrespective of variation in their social, cultural, or personal characteristics: a notion that came to be referred to as procedural objectivity (Eisner 1992, see also Newell 1986).[4] Ruled out here are appeals to intuition, or to forms of expertise that are unique to a particular person or type of person. Reliance upon explicit or 'transparent' procedures was also seen as providing the basis for other researchers to replicate an initial study. And replication was regarded by many positivists as essential in order to test whether the knowledge produced is sound, precisely to show that it had not been affected by the 'subjectivity' of the researcher.

Central to positivism was a refusal to extend knowledge claims beyond those that could be fully supported by evidence of this kind, an attitude that has sometimes been given the closely related label 'empiricism'. Indeed, the two words – 'positivism' and 'empiricism' – are often treated as synonyms. This kind of empiricism had two important implications.

First, it ruled out those areas of inquiry that were seen as offering no prospect of empirical evidence of the required kind. These included not

3 Interestingly, this was at odds with the outlook of Comte, see Scharff (1995).

4 For evidence that this developed only slowly and by no means straightforwardly in natural science see Shapin (1994) and Daston and Garrison (2007).

just theology and ethics,[5] but also sometimes social science too, since some positivists believed that knowledge is available only at the level of the description of physical behaviour, in the manner of psychological behaviourism, so that any appeal to intentions, attitudes, and thoughts, etc., or to unobservable entities like social institutions, was judged to be beyond the reach of rigorous analysis.

Secondly, empiricism insists that even in those fields where knowledge *is* judged to be possible, research must be strictly limited to questions for which the necessary kind of evidence is currently available. Speculation – knowledge claims not effectively supported by such evidence – must be avoided.

There has, however, been variation in what we might call the severity of the empiricism adopted by positivists, in other words in how narrowly they define the domain of legitimate evidence, and in the restrictions they place upon what kinds of inference can be used to draw justified conclusions. As we have already seen, a very stringent version, modeled on physics, insisted that the only legitimate data are those produced by explicitly defined procedures designed to measure observable phenomena that can be subjected to experimental manipulation, with the only valid product being universal laws. On this basis, not just qualitative, but also most quantitative, social science would be ruled out as unscientific, since it is unable to apply the strong form of measurement characteristic of natural science, can use only non-experimental designs, and at best produces only low-level, probabilistic generalizations. Not surprisingly, most quantitative researchers have adopted a more liberal definition of scientific method, one that legitimates various kinds of *approximation* to the physics model in these three respects.

Furthermore, it should be stressed that there is no automatic connection between positivism and the use of quantitative methods. For one thing, many quantitative researchers deny that they are positivists (see, for example, Marsh 1979). Conversely, we should note that empiricism had an important influence on the early development of *qualitative* methods, albeit usually reinforced by other influences. Thus, modern anthropology is often dated from Malinowski's insistence that ethnographers must collect their own data through direct observation rather than relying upon

---

5 Values came to be interpreted by many positivists as no more than expressions of emotional attitude 'for' or 'against' something.

'travellers' tales'; and the influence upon him of positivist ideas has been documented (Leach 1957). We can also see the effect of empiricism today not just in the continuing commitment of ethnographers to participant observation, to 'being there' (Geertz 1988), but also in their felt need to carefully record data, whether via fieldnotes or transcription of electronic recordings, to check the testimony from informants, and to provide evidence in their research reports. Moreover, some qualitative researchers, especially discourse analysts, insist that data must be audio- or video recorded, on the grounds that this provides a more accurate and detailed record than fieldnotes; that these recordings must be transcribed in order to capture not just *what* was said but also *how* it was said; and that all the data should be made available to readers so as to allow replication of the analysis (Peräkylä 2003). Alongside this, they frequently insist that the analysis must not go beyond the data, perhaps even that it should be restricted to what is 'observable' *in* the data (Schegloff 1997).

It is easy to forget how radical an orientation positivism was in earlier times, and how radical it still is today in some contexts: it challenges religious claims to knowledge about the world, various kinds of speculative philosophy that do not pay close attention to what could be warranted by empirical evidence, and even any appeal to what is 'obvious' in commonsense terms. It was often promoted as a 'levelling' orientation that opens up knowledge to anyone willing and able to employ scientific method, and we can see this in current arguments about the importance of evidence-based practice in medicine and other fields (for instance Oakley 2000). Furthermore, positivism often involved the expectation that science, including the human sciences, would pave the way for substantial social and political progress: by undermining beliefs and practices that were based solely on partial interests, superstition or tradition ('folk wisdom'), replacing these with ones founded on scientific evidence that (it was believed) would be in everyone's interests. The role of natural science in stimulating technological progress in the eighteenth and nineteenth centuries was taken as confirming this vision.

In short, then, positivism had considerable influence upon social researchers over the course of the first half of the twentieth century. It stimulated the emergence of quantitative method, but aspects of it also shaped early forms of qualitative work; and it continues to have a subterranean influence even today, especially where it is reinforced by other methodological philosophies. However, in the second part of the twentieth century there was increasing criticism of positivist ideas, with various alternative philosophies being promoted. Some of these were almost as old as positivism itself: one of the earliest was what has been called interpretivism.

Interpretivism

The conflict between positivist and interpretivist ideas can be traced back into the nineteenth century. At this time, especially in Germany, there developed influential arguments to the effect that a distinctive kind of scientific method is required in studying history and the social sciences, one that is very different from that characteristic of physics and the other natural sciences (see Hammersley 1989: ch.1). Along these lines, interpretivists argued that in studying the social world it is essential to draw upon our human capacity to understand fellow human beings 'from the inside' – through empathy, shared experience and culture, etc – rather than solely from the outside in the way that we are forced to try to explain the behaviour of physical objects. One of the several words for 'understanding' available in the German language – Verstehen – came to be used to refer to this capacity. Indeed, it was often argued that Verstehen provides deeper knowledge of human phenomena than we can ever gain of the physical world (Truzzi 1974; Outhwaite 1976; Hausheer 1996; Harrington 2000).

Interpretivism was often associated with an insistence on the fundamental differences in nature between the phenomena investigated by the natural sciences and those studied by historians and social scientists. The key difference is that people – unlike atoms, chemicals, and even most non-human forms of life – actively interpret or make sense of their environment and of themselves; that the ways in which they do this are shaped by the particular cultures in which they live; and that these distinctive cultural orientations will strongly influence not only what they believe but also what they do. Thus, diverse ways of life, and associated beliefs about the world, can be found, both at different points in history *and* coexisting (peacefully or in conflict) at any one time across various societies, and even within the same society. The task of the social scientist, from the interpretivist point of view, is to document these cultures, and perhaps also their sources and consequences. However, as already indicated, it is believed that this cannot be done through the kind of science advocated by positivists. Instead, researchers must try to understand other cultures by suspending their own cultural assumptions as far as this is possible, and learning the ways of thinking and feeling, and modes of action, characteristic of the culture they are investigating.

We can see, then, how interpretivism rejects central tenets of positivism. Interpretivists argue that we cannot understand why people do what they do, or why particular institutions exist and operate in characteristic ways, without grasping how people interpret and make sense of their world and act on their interpretations: in other words, without understanding the distinctive cultural character of their beliefs, attitudes, and practices, how these have developed over time, and/or how they ongoingly generate the social world. Moreover, to achieve this understanding, we must draw upon our own social experience or capacity for learning, rather than seeking to achieve procedural objectivity. And, from this point of view, any attempt to find universal causal relationships grounded in some fixed human nature or form of society is futile. Instead, the primary focus must be on trying to understand particular people and events in specific socio-historical circumstances. This is sometimes labeled as an idiographic focus, as against positivism's concern with nomothetic knowledge – with knowledge of universal, timeless laws.

One interpretivist way of thinking about the kind of understanding required in social science derives from hermeneutics. This had its origins in attempts to decipher the meanings conveyed by ancient texts, such as those of the Greeks and the Romans and biblical sources. For some historians and social scientists in the nineteenth century, this discipline became the model for the socio-historical sciences, and this continued long into the twentieth-century (Palmer 1969; Taylor 1985: ch.1). For example, in a famous characterization of the task of ethnography, the anthropologist Clifford Geertz (1973: 10) described it as amounting to constructing a reading of a manuscript that is 'foreign, faded, and full of ellipses, incoherencies, suspicious emendations and tendentious commentaries'.

Another important strand of thinking within interpretivism derives from the phenomenological movement in philosophy. This argued that all knowledge of the world, including science, is grounded in processes of immediate experience, and that these processes need to be subjected to careful description. Moreover, this must be done in ways that avoid, as far as possible, the distortions that can be produced by prior conceptual presuppositions. Such presuppositions must be suspended, and careful attention given to the character of phenomena as they appear in our experience.[6]

Some psychologists and social scientists drew the conclusion from phenomenology that, instead of taking commonsense knowledge of the world for granted as a basis for social science, or simply dismissing it as defective in the manner of positivism, we should instead explore how it comes to take the form that it does, and indeed how the psychological and social phenomena people experience are constituted and sustained through the processes of interpretation and social interaction in which they engage (see, for example, Berger and Luckmann 1967). At the same time there was also an emphasis on cultural variation in these constitutive processes – among individuals, groups, and communities. The influence of phenomenology reinforced the primary focus of some qualitative researchers on detailed description of the experience and perspectives of diverse groups of people.

Both nineteenth-century hermeneutics and phenomenology proposed distinctive methods of investigation that their advocates claimed were just as rigorous as the very different kind of method employed by natural science. A third philosophical movement that strongly influenced the development of qualitative methods in US sociology in the first half of the twentieth century was pragmatism (Hammersley 1989: ch.2). This took a somewhat different line from the two other movements I have discussed. Pragmatism drew no sharp distinction between natural and social science, but insisted instead on a generic formulation of scientific inquiry that downplayed its differences from commonsense thinking in everyday life.[7]

However, in the twentieth century the commitment of interpretivism to some alternative, equally rigorous, method began to change. Under the influence of Heidegger's reformulation of phenomenology, Gadamer's philosophical hermeneutics, and Rorty's reinterpretation of pragmatism, it came to be argued that understanding other people is necessarily an uncertain process that relies upon openness to the world, and on the exercise of personal capacities, especially the imagination, *rather than upon any method*. Thus, Gadamer argued that knowledge is always generated in

6 On phenomenology, see Moran (2002). For its application in social and psychological research see Schutz (1962), Berger and Luckmann (1967), Giorgi and Giorgi (2008) and Smith and Osborn (2008).

7 On pragmatism, see, for example, De Waal (2005).

particular socio-historical contexts and must draw on the resources these provide, it cannot rely upon an abstract, scientific method, even of the kind identified by nineteenth-century hermeneutics or early phenomenology. Strong parallels were drawn here with the kind of understanding of life characteristic of literature and art.

In summary, then, interpretivism carries a range of implications for research. First, it requires the researcher to adopt an exploratory orientation, and in particular to learn to understand the distinctive perspectives of the people involved, and perhaps also to observe how their patterns of action unfold in particular contexts. Above all, any tendency to dismiss other people's attitudes or behaviour as irrational, or as objectionable in some other way, must be resisted: instead, research must be carried out on the assumption that their attitudes and behaviour make sense to, and are seen as justifiable by, them, with the researcher suspending any evaluation. The aim is to discover the 'logic' or rationality of what may at first seem strange, illogical, or even evil; and this requires detailed exploration of people's experience and perspectives. This, it is argued, is an essential requirement not just for explaining but even for *describing* people's behaviour and the social institutions in which it is located, and which it helps sustain. Many of the studies listed in Box 1.1 reflect the influence of interpretivism, but perhaps especially those of Morton, Bogdan, and Mitchell.

Interpretivism was one type of methodological philosophy that came to challenge positivism and quantitative method in social science in the middle of the twentieth century, and it had a huge impact on qualitative research. However, there was another, rather different, tradition that was at least as influential during the same period, what is often referred to as 'critical' theory and research.[8]

The 'critical' tradition

As with positivism and interpretivism, the immediate origins of 'critical' research lie in the nineteenth century, this time in the philosophical work of Hegel and Marx. Prior to this, Kant had written three 'critiques', the first of which was concerned with identifying the limits of human knowledge.

8 I have put 'critical' in quote marks because the meaning here goes beyond the sense in which all researchers adopt a critical orientation in assessing knowledge claims. See Hammersley (1992: ch.6) and (1995: ch.2).

In the case of Hegel and Marx the scope for critique was extended to include social institutions and practices, along with the forms of knowledge associated with these.

The most obvious way in which a 'critical' orientation contrasts with both positivism and interpretivism is that whereas they are concerned solely with identifying causal patterns and/or documenting other people's perspectives and practices, 'critical' researchers also evaluate the phenomena, such as people and institutions, they study. They do this either in terms of some set of ideals built into their own political or ethical position or against standards that they identify as inherent within the sociocultural contexts they are examining (this second approach is sometimes referred to as 'immanent' or 'internal' critique). So, their research involves evaluative as well as factual concepts – for example 'exploitation', 'oppression', 'emancipation' – and is seen as properly directed towards achieving particular kinds of political goal: reducing or eliminating exploitation and oppression, and bringing about emancipation.

Equally important, whereas interpretivism aims to a large extent at understanding other cultures 'in their own terms', 'critical' research usually insists that they can be properly understood only within the framework of a global theory that locates them in a wider social system and/or a larger process of historical development that has been properly theorized. And, like some positivists but unlike interpretivists, 'critical' researchers insist that people's behaviour will often need to be explained by factors that are beyond their awareness. Indeed, they argue that in many cases this awareness will have been systematically distorted by social processes.

These three methodological philosophies also involve very different attitudes towards history. Positivists tend to treat the ideas of the past, where these are not regarded as precursors of present-day scientific knowledge, as wrong-headed – as the product of bias or irrationality.[9] By contrast, some interpretivists reject any notion of historical progress, viewing the past as consisting of different eras, each with its own distinctive worldview; and they believe that these worldviews cannot be evaluated against one another because there is no overarching cultural scheme within which this could be done. 'Critical' research shares something with each of the other philosophies in this respect, but also differs significantly.

9 Interestingly, once again this was not the view of Comte, see Scharff (1995).

Hegel, whose philosophical work is one of the key sources for the 'critical' tradition, rejected the positivist idea that there could be any major set of beliefs or cultural assumptions in the past that was simply false, the product of irrationality. In this he was in line with the interpretivists. However, like the positivists, he saw the past as leading up to the present, albeit in a dialectical rather than a linear fashion. What he meant by this was that historical progress is achieved by struggle between different worldviews, on the model of a debate, with this struggle leading in each era to the emergence of a new perspective that transcends previous ones (incorporating and transforming elements from each of them), which itself then comes to dominate. However, the same process begins again in the next historical era: an opposing worldview will develop, leading to further struggle, with these conflicting perspectives themselves subsequently being transcended. Furthermore, the worldviews involved here are not just sets of ideas but whole ways of life: cultures embodied within particular societies. Thus, Hegel traces the process of dialectical development in terms of ancient Greece against Rome, medieval versus early modern society, and so on.

Hegel did not believe that this process of historical development would go on forever. Rather, he saw it as coming to an end at a point where not only true knowledge but also all genuine human ideals would be realized, and previous conflicts among them resolved. He claimed that this point had more or less been reached in the early nineteenth century, and that his own philosophy was therefore the final one that, at least potentially, captured the whole truth about the world.

Marx gave an important twist to Hegel's philosophical system, seeking to transform it into a scientific theory of society. While he inherited much of what I have just outlined, he differed from Hegel in seeing the driving force of history not as the conflict between ideas but rather as one between different social classes. And the character of this conflict at any point in time reflected the stage of historical development that had been reached, this being primarily determined by the development of productive economic forces. In other words, the conflict in ideas, or ideologies, stemmed from social class divisions and struggle generated by particular modes of production, not the other way round. And Marx saw the rise and fall of social classes as being determined by the socio-economic development of societies: for example, by the move from hunting and gathering societies to peasant forms of production, controlled by landlords, through to the rise of modern, industrial capitalism in the nineteenth century, associated with the emergence of the bourgeoisie as the dominant class and the proletariat as the main subordinate class.

Like Hegel, Marx believed that the process of historical development would come to an end, and that at that point human ideals, including our knowledge of the world, would be realized. However, for him this had not yet happened, and it required substantial social transformation. It would only take place in the future, though he believed that this would be in the *near* future: when the industrial working class overthrew capitalism and established a communist society.

An implication of Marx's argument is that in order to understand any particular situation one must locate it within a broader understanding of the current stage of development of the society in which it occurs, and the history of that society. This has very important implications for the practice of social inquiry. For one thing, it means that a comprehensive theory of society is required, as against a more specific disciplinary perspective or focus on a particular social problem. Equally important, it implies that the researcher is not located outside of the socio-historical process but is necessarily part of, and shaped by, it. As a result, he or she cannot but operate within some perspective that has been generated by the process of social development, and this carries with it the dangers of bias, and therefore error, *but also the only potential for true understanding that is available.*

Marx claimed that a distinctive set of interests, and a distinctive set of ideas related to them (an ideology), belonged to each social class. Furthermore, he argued that it was the responsibility of the intellectual to align her or himself with whatever class is the most progressive one in current society; and in the case of nineteenth-century Europe this was the working class. Marx saw such commitment as ethically required in that intellectual work has value only when it is engaged with the process of social change.[10] The idea that research can be detached from ethical and political concerns, that it can or should try to be 'value neutral', in the manner proposed by most forms of positivism and interpretivism, is

---

10 An important parallel tradition here is that of action research, itself diverse but generally sharing a commitment to practical engagement, see Reason and Bradbury (2001).

dismissed by 'critical' researchers as either an ideological disguise or as self-delusion.

Marx also saw such political commitment as providing the only chance of gaining a true understanding of the world, both of the present and of the past. This was because he believed that it is the progressive social class, the one that is destined to come to power next, that has the best motive and opportunity for gaining a true understanding of the world.[11] According to Marx, once a social class has become dominant, its perspective on the world, while containing some original truths, will start to be distorted by the need to hold on to power in socio-economic conditions that are increasingly disadvantageous for it; and he assumed that false ideas would be most effective in this task, since true ideas would point to the need for this class to be overthrown. The only exception was the case of the working class, precisely because he saw its coming to power as bringing the process of historical development to an end, as establishing a classless society in which human ideals – including true knowledge of the world – would be realized.

Despite this standpoint epistemology, Marx did also insist on the need for scientific analysis: he did not believe that the spontaneously developed understandings of working class people were automatically valid, not least because they are likely to be shaped by ideology. For this reason, ideology-critique became central to the subsequent development of Western Marxism (Jay 1996). Dominant ideas were seen as legitimating the *status quo*, often through portraying it as natural and unchangeable. Indeed, it was argued by Marx that social formations inherently generate false appearances that are taken by most people to be reality. Thus, undermining the dominant ideology through critique came to be viewed as a precondition for significant change, and a major responsibility for intellectuals – a category to which social researchers would clearly belong.

'Critical' researchers today inherit many of the ideas outlined above, though they have abandoned, or downplay, others. One change is that, often, the focus is no longer primarily on social class inequalities and conflicts but on other kinds of social division as well or instead, notably those surrounding gender, race and ethnicity, sexuality, and disability.

11 This is a form of what has come to be called 'standpoint epistemology', later championed in a revised form by some feminists: see Hartsock (1987) and for an overview Anderson (2011).

Whereas traditional Marxists would see these other forms of division as ultimately deriving from social class differences, and as being abolished at the same time that social class inequality is overcome, most 'critical' researchers today treat them as having at least the same importance, and as being independent of, and just as fundamental as, social class. As part of this, many 'critical' researchers have abandoned the particular global theory and meta-narrative developed by Marx, and either replaced it with a new one or adopted a narrower and more specific orientation focused on bringing about particular sorts of social change related to the kind of social division with which they are primarily concerned.

Despite these changes in the 'critical' tradition, what is usually retained is the idea that research should operate within a framework of political assumptions, and should be geared to serving political goals. Many feminists, for example, believe that their research must be primarily directed towards the emancipation of women, though some – socialist feminists – insist that this must be done in association with class struggle. Almost all 'critical' researchers believe that researchers have a responsibility to resist dominant ideologies and to challenge inequitable social relations through their research.

In carrying out his analysis of capitalism, Marx drew on quantitative as well as qualitative data, but most 'critical' research in the twentieth century, and more recently, has adopted a more qualitative approach. For instance there has been a very influential tradition of Marxist historiography, as well as substantial ethnographic work and interview studies inspired by the 'critical' tradition, especially by social movements like feminism, anti-racism, and disability activism. Nevertheless, there has been some significant Marxist work of a quantitative kind (see for example Wright 1979) and some discussion among Marxists about the relationship between quantitative and qualitative approaches (see Burawoy 1987; Morrow 1994: ch.8). The studies by Rai, Wacquant, and Wetherell and Edley in Box 1.1 have been influenced by the 'critical' tradition in key respects.

As noted earlier, the philosophical ideas behind both the interpretivist and the 'critical' traditions have their origins for the most part in the nineteenth century. The final philosophical approach we will look at emerged more recently, and it amounts to a significant reaction against the others, though some of its ideas are inherited from them. It also revives some even older ideas, notably from ancient scepticism.

Constructionism

This final type of methodological philosophy is even broader and more diverse than the other three. The word 'constructionism', or 'constructivism', has become widely used in social science over the past twenty or thirty years. While it has been employed to refer to a range of rather different ideas, it is possible to outline a few core assumptions.[12]

What is central, first of all, is rejection of any idea that cognition, or even perception, is a process whereby objects and their characteristics, existing in the world, impress themselves upon our understanding. Instead, it is argued that perception and cognition are active processes, in which anything apparently 'given' is actually a product of processes of selection and construction. Another key theme is that these processes are socio-cultural in character, with different cultures generating divergent experiential worlds and stocks of 'knowledge'. This is, of course, similar to interpretivism, but there remain important differences. In particular, constructionists often question whether understanding other people, and perhaps even oneself, is ever possible. They also suggest that multiple, incommensurable interpretations are frequently generated and circulate within the same contexts.

The two key ideas that I have identified as central to constructionism up to this point are compatible, in principle, with the notion that through perception and cognition the intrinsic, independent features of objects and events in the world, and the principles upon which they operate, can be understood (see Maxwell 2012: ch.1). However, much constructionism goes beyond this to suggest that the character and content of any 'knowledge' and 'understanding' reflects primarily, or perhaps even entirely, the nature of the construction process, including the features, dispositions, etc of the agent involved. In other words, it is denied that knowledge can correspond to the intrinsic character of a set of independently existing objects.

This sceptical idea, whose history can be traced back to ancient philosophy (Hankinson 1998), has important implications for how inquiry should be pursued. The task can no longer be to document the features of various types of object existing in the world – their relationships, causes and consequences, etc. It is insisted that we must not be misled by appearances

12 Advocates of some forms of work I am including under the heading of constructionism would resist that label. See, for instance, Button and Sharrock (1992). For a general introduction to constructionism/constructivism, see Burr 2003 and 2004.

into forgetting that such objects owe their existence and their 'character' to the constitutive processes that generated them. Instead, the proper focus of study must be those processes themselves. As should be clear, this involves a major shift, or re-specification, of the goal of scientific inquiry. An example would be to treat people's personal characteristics not as intrinsic to them but rather to examine the discursive practices through which people are characterized as intelligent/stupid, motivated/lazy, confident/hesitant, and so on; and how these operate in particular contexts, from informal situations among friends or family to more institutional ones such as job interviews or psychiatric assessments.[13]

There is another feature of constructionism that adds further complexity. Some versions of it do not view social phenomena as being constructed through the perceptual and cognitive dispositions of individuals who each independently make sense of their environment. Rather, the construction of social worlds is seen as occuring through shared processes of communication and social interaction; it is *these* processes that are constitutive of the character of social phenomena rather than the perceptual and cognitive capabilities of individuals. Indeed, for some constructionists the very existence of individuals with particular identities is itself only constituted in and through socio-cultural processes, whether those associated with particular, occasioned patterns of social interaction or those generated by relatively large-scale socio-historical formations that produce distinctive forms of discourse. I will call this more complex position, itself displaying several varieties, *social* constructionism.

We can identify at least two major stances within social constructionism, as it relates to qualitative research. The most common one involves a focus on studying the methods or practices through which people collectively construct their shared worlds. Key examples of this stance can be found in various forms of discourse analysis, where the goal is to document discursive practices or broader discursive formations that are seen as constitutive of social phenomena. There can be differences here in what is taken to be a discursive practice, in what is regarded as legitimate and sufficient evidence, and no doubt in other respects too. But what is shared is the idea that by means of discourse analysis the character of the practices through which social phenomena are constituted

13 For a discussion of 'discursive psychology', see Edwards and Potter (1992), Edwards (1997 and 2005).

can be documented (see, for example, Wetherell *et al.* 2001). The studies mentioned in Box 1.1 by MacLure and Walker, Wetherell and Edley, and Levitas are examples of this sort of approach.

Often, this has been associated with an argument that all language-use is performative, in the sense that it is not simply concerned (or concerned at all) with representing the world, with 'getting the facts straight', but is primarily if not exclusively directed at performing actions *within* the world. Thus, some commentators have stressed the rhetorical character of all accounts; in other words, that even when they *appear* to be concerned solely with description or explanation they are inevitably aimed at persuading audiences. One implication of this is that different people will inevitably produce conflicting accounts of the same scene, depending upon their assumptions, interests and purposes.[14] With much the same result, other researchers have noted that accounts often take the form of narratives, and that the same set of events can be narrated in many different ways, leading to divergent versions of what happened.[15]

A second, rather different, form of social constructionism questions the idea, built into the first one, that the analyst can document the character and properties of discursive practices, or other sorts of practice, in some rigorous analytic manner. It is objected that this treats these practices as if they existed independently of the constitutive practices employed by the analyst her or himself. It is insisted, instead, that all researchers are necessarily implicated in the processes whereby social phenomena are constructed, and cannot escape this. It is also sometimes argued that the task of the analyst should be to subvert whatever seems to be the dominant constitutive regime in order to open up the prospect of something new, or to seek to identify and encourage novel or resistant forms.[16]

There are many sources of constructionist ideas. Indeed, as I noted earlier, some are even to be found within positivism, interpretivism, and

14 For examples of work along these lines, see Pollner (1987), Potter (1996), Cuff (1993) and Taylor and Littleton (2006).

15 For an enjoyable historical exploration of narrative variation, tracing the telling and retelling of an eighteenth-century murder story, see Brewer (2004).

16 There are also versions in which any distinction between agent, whether participant or analyst, and passive objects on which they act is erased, in favour of a view which presents objects of many kinds as involved in mutually constituting relationships that generate complex, contingent, and changing patterns. For an exploration of the implications of this sort of view for research method, see Law (2004).

the 'critical' tradition. For example, seventeenth century empiricism drew a distinction between primary and secondary characteristics of physical objects, with the latter – for example colour – being dependent upon human perceptual capabilities rather than being intrinsic features of objects (Murphy *et al.* 1998). Similarly, as we saw, phenomenology was concerned with how experience is constituted through subjective processes, rather than being the result of a direct apprehension of the world. And we also noted that a central idea of 'critical' research is that the dominant ideology emerges out of existing social circumstances and is taken for granted by most people – indeed, treated as 'natural' – obscuring the fact that those circumstances are a socio-historical product and can be changed.

However, prior to the second half of the twentieth century, none of these ideas were fully developed within social science into the kinds of constructionism I have outlined. One major stimulus for this development was the work of the philosopher of science Thomas Kuhn (1970).[17] He challenged the positivist idea that twentieth-century physics represented a cumulative development from earlier work in that discipline, such as that of Newton. Instead, he suggested that it was incommensurable with what had gone before: in other words that at the time it emerged there was no common ground on which these two versions of physics could be compared and evaluated. Here, Kuhn laid emphasis on the social and cultural character of natural science research. He argued that, rather than being a process of logically deriving knowledge from empirical evidence, it necessarily relies upon concepts shared within research communities existing in particular times and places, concepts that are open-ended in character but anchored by exemplary studies recognized as such by the relevant community. These concepts and exemplars make up what he refers to as a paradigm, and this provides a framework of assumptions which both indicates what is already known and contains 'puzzles' that require further work.

Kuhn saw mature sciences like physics, or particular fields within them, as being dominated during any one period by one single paradigm. However, over time some of the puzzles within the paradigm would come to prove recalcitrant and be recognized as 'anomalies', at which point there was the potential for a 'scientific revolution' that could eventually lead to

17 For detailed discussion of his work, see Bird (2000) and Sharrock and Read (2002).

the adoption of a new paradigm; for example, the move from Newtonian to twentieth-century physics.

In short, what Kuhn offered was a very different picture of natural science from the previously common view, adopted both by positivists and by many interpretivists: that natural scientific knowledge gradually accumulates, with errors being corrected, and new discoveries adding to further knowledge. Instead, according to Kuhn, the process of development is discontinuous, punctuated by paradigmatic revolutions involving disagreement that cannot be resolved at the time by rational means.

It is worth noting that Kuhn specifically describes social science as being in a pre-paradigmatic, or non-paradigmatic, state, *precisely because it continuously displays a host of competing approaches*. However, in appropriating his work social scientists tended to treat their own approaches as competing scientific paradigms. Moreover, his ideas were taken to raise fundamental questions about the status of the accounts of social scientists themselves – it reinforced the idea that these should be viewed as constructions generated by particular paradigmatic assumptions none of which could claim epistemological privilege over others.

Here we can see one important respect in which constructionism breaks with interpretivism, perhaps throwing into doubt the very possibility of knowledge in the conventional sense of that term. And there is significant overlap here with those ideas, deriving from French twentieth-century philosophy, that are often placed under the headings of post-structuralism and postmodernism, and which were very influential in the latter decades of the twentieth century. These challenge many attitudes that are regarded as characteristic of the modern world (often traced back to the Enlightenment) – such as belief in the validity, value, and power of scientific knowledge and in the prospect of progress, both in the sphere of knowledge and in social, economic and political life. However, postmodernism tends to involve not a simple rejection of modernism but rather a refusal to treat what it stands for as privileged as against what it opposes. Instead, there is a commitment to holding opposites in tension, on the grounds that there is no basis for deciding between them.[18]

One of the sources on which Kuhn drew was the work of the French philosophers and historians of science Gaston Bachelard and Georges

18 Again, there is a parallel here with the attitudes of some ancient sceptics, see Vogt (2010).

Canguilhem. These writers also saw the development of scientific fields as marked by discontinuity, in which new problematics (frameworks of assumptions organised around some set of problems to be investigated) arose to replace older ones. Moreover, they denied that there was any substantial unity of theoretical and methodological assumption across the various fields of modern natural science, and refused to treat any of them, including physics, as methodologically exemplary. Instead, they stressed the discontinuities *among* scientific fields, as well as those occurring in the development of particular fields over time as new problematics emerged to replace previously influential ones. Where, prior to this, it had often been assumed, for example by positivism and pragmatism, that there was a unitary scientific method, these writers emphasized variation in the methods of the different sciences.

These French explorations in the history and philosophy of science were among the main influences on the work of Michel Foucault (see Gutting 1989), who has come to be identified by many as a key figure in postmodernism (though he himself did not accept the label). He investigated how the human sciences – notably psychology, medicine and criminology – developed in discontinuous ways, and especially how they became embedded in specific institutional practices that have come to constitute modern social life. For instance, he traced what he saw as a transformation in the treatment of madness between the sixteenth and nineteenth centuries. Working with detailed historical data of many kinds, he sought to identify the distinctive discourses, texts and networks of power relations that dominated different periods, and how these generated various kinds of occupational and organizational practice, accompanied by their own 'truth regimes', these defining the identities and constituting the perceptions and actions of those involved. For Foucault there were sharp discontinuities between different epochs in these terms, characterized by very different types of discursive construction and institutional practice. And the task he took on was to document these; though he also saw his work as providing tools for political struggles, for example that around the rights of prisoners (see Foucault and Deleuze 1977; Macey 1993: 256–89; Miller 1993: 187–94).[19]

19 His work has stimulated distinctive forms of discourse analysis, see Macdonell (1986) and Howarth (2000).

Other important stimuli to constructionism in continental Europe were the movements of twentieth-century thought referred to as structuralism and post-structuralism. It is not possible clearly to separate these from one another since, once again, the label 'post' indicates a process of elaboration and change rather than a complete abandonment of the earlier position – so that post-structuralism inherits important assumptions from structuralism.

Structuralism had its origins in the work of the Swiss linguist Ferdinand de Saussure. He transformed the study of language in the late nineteenth century by shifting the main focus away from tracing the development of particular languages, and how words and other language elements had changed over time, to an interest in the structural character of languages as they exist and operate at any one point in time: in particular, how they generate distinctive yet intelligible patterns of sound and meaning. He explained this capacity as resulting from the deployment of structural contrasts between specific sounds, words, and grammatical forms. For example, at a phonemic level, in English the difference between the words 'cat', 'cut', and 'cot' all hinge on contrasts in vowel sounds that are by no means always significant in other languages. In semantics, the terms for colours used in different languages divide up the spectrum in varying ways, *each term gaining its sense from how it relates to the others*. The key point is that meaning is generated *within* the system of language, words do not get their sense from pre-existing objects to which they refer, nor from the intentions of the speaker or writer. This sort of structuralist approach became the dominant one in linguistics in the twentieth century, and its influence spread much more widely into the study of literature, anthropology, and even psychoanalysis and Marxism.

An important feature of structuralism was its commitment to science, albeit in a form that was not modeled on physics or any other natural science. Within linguistics, this demanded careful and detailed attention to linguistic material in order to detect relatively simple underlying generative structures made up of significant contrasts. Sometimes these structures were seen as unique to particular languages, so that it was often concluded that languages construct the world in discrepant ways; but there were also attempts to find universal forms (most notably in the highly influential work of Chomsky). Either way, these generative structures served a similar function within the structuralist project as the assumption of fixed universal laws did in positivism. Moreover, this distinctive conception of science influenced some forms of qualitative research, most notably within anthropology through the work of Lévi-Strauss and the practitioners of cognitive anthropology (Tyler 1969), as exemplified by Frake's study mentioned in Chapter 1. The general trend in the later decades of the twentieth century was, however, to question structuralism's assumptions about science, and this was central to much post-structuralism.

The idea, central to structuralism, that signs are not natural in character but matters of cultural convention, and are in that sense arbitrary, was capitalized upon by a number of French writers, most notably Roland Barthes (see Culler 2002). He stimulated much work in cultural studies by applying it to aspects of popular culture. One example he used was all-in wrestling, arguing that this sport amounts to the exchange of symbols rather than to the expression of natural aggression. Indeed, he suggests that it relies upon a kind of authentic but knowing pretense on the part of both the wrestlers themselves and their audiences. The latter, as with any kind of theatre, are required willingly to suspend disbelief: treating as real what is known to be contrived. The key point for Barthes is, however, that there is no reality that is *not* contrived or constructed in-and-through social and discursive practices. In this way, he developed structuralist ideas in a radical direction that stimulated a considerable body of empirical research, under the heading of semiotics (see Bignell 1997).

Another influential writer often associated with post-structuralism and postmodernism, but also rejecting these labels, was Jacques Derrida. He started from a critique of phenomenological philosophy, charging that it treated language as anchored in a direct relationship to the world (concept to object, sound to meaning), and as having a stable structure that thereby produced fixed, essential meanings accessible to anyone who knows the language. By contrast, Derrida emphasized the extent to which structures, whether within languages or within particular texts, involve conflicting and shifting elements. As a result, meaning always escapes our grasp even while we nevertheless manage to communicate with others, feeling that we understand what they say or write. Indeed, a key feature of much post-structuralism and postmodernism is a denial that language or discourse can be a tool that is under our control. Rather, it is claimed, discourse forms us, and in a sense even speaks through us.

The writer who applied the term 'postmodernism' to his own work, Jean-Francois Lyotard, emphasized that we must think of discourses not so much as languages but as language games: as forms of practice that generate meaning, and that are incommensurable with one another.[20] As this indicates, what postmodernism opposes above all is the idea that there is, or can be, a single comprehensive perspective in terms of which we should understand or approach the world, whether that of science or of 'critical' philosophy. Instead, it is argued that any particular discourse leaves untouched an elusive remainder, some of which may be central for other discourses. This means that we must recognize and accept radical diversity in perspective. Moreover, the opposition to purportedly 'totalising' perspectives here is not just on epistemological or ontological grounds, but also on ethical and political ones: it is argued that such perspectives are totalitarian in political terms, and have generated social oppression, for example the imprisonment of political opponents in mental hospitals and in the gulag in Eastern Europe during the twentieth century.

While belonging to the political Left, many of the French writers associated with post-structuralism and postmodernism were reacting directly against Marxism, with its claim to know that history is leading to a society in which all divisions will be overcome. The challenge here was not just to any idea of historical inevitability (Berlin 1954; Popper 1957) but also to the very idea that such a trend would be desirable. Rather, it was seen as likely to erase or overlook important differences in identity and experience. This line of thinking parallels developments within the study of gender, ethnicity, sexuality, and disability, where there has been an ongoing conflict between a refusal to treat these sources of difference as biological in character (this being dismissed as 'essentialism') and the insistence that they are nevertheless fundamental and must be recognized and valued for themselves.

I have emphasized the diverse ideas to be found under the heading of constructionism.[21] These have been very influential among qualitative researchers in the past few decades. In particular, they have stimulated research on text, discourse, narrative, and images. Much of this work has been designed to examine in detail how the use of symbols, broadly

---

20 He took the concept of language games from the philosopher Wittgenstein, whose work has also influenced other social scientists drawing on interpretivism and constructionism. See, for instance, Hutchinson *et al.*, 2008.

21 And there have been other important sources, even within France, that I have not mentioned: from the work of Deleuze to that of Latour. See Gutting (2011), James (2012), Harman (2009), and Restivo (2010).

conceived, actively constitutes psychological and social phenomena, constructing them in *some* ways rather than others, and generating diversity or fragmentation. This work has also sometimes been closely related to a political concern with what is seen as cultural imperialism (Clifford and Marcus 1986). As part of this, there has been a shift in some quarters from viewing science as a progressive force to seeing it as an expression of Western political and economic dominance; with some writers defending, as an alternative, modes of knowing that are marginalized, for example those of 'indigenous' groups (see Denzin *et al.* 2008).

Moreover, as we saw, there are forms of constructionist research that are not concerned simply with documenting how psychological and social phenomena are constructed through the discourses and practices operating within particular situations, but rather with how research accounts themselves are implicated in this. Indeed, there has been a small body of work that has applied discourse and narrative analysis to research reports, especially to those of qualitative researchers (see Hammersley 1994). Beyond this, there have been calls for researchers to display a reflexive awareness of how they simultaneously document and construct the world through studying it, and how this betrays their own commitments and orientations. As a result, constructionism has sometimes stimulated forms of research writing that are specifically designed to undercut not only the scientific image of research but also any claim on its behalf to well-established knowledge (see, for instance, Ashmore 1989).

Summary

In this chapter we have looked at some of the methodological philosophies that have shaped qualitative research. We started with positivism, which was a major influence on quantitative research; though we also noted respects in which it had shaped qualitative work as well. We moved on to interpretivism, which has been among the most important sets of ideas underpinning qualitative enquiry. It stresses cultural difference, while insisting that understanding can take place across cultures. We noted how in some of its forms interpretivism proposed an alternative conception of rigorous inquiry to that ascribed to natural science by positivism, while other forms rejected any idea of reliance upon method, and especially scientific method. A third set of philosophical ideas, collected together under the heading of 'critical' philosophy, shares some features with both positivism and interpretivism, but also differs significantly from both – notably in its emphasis on the need for a comprehensive theoretical framework and explicit social critique, and on the inevitability of political engagement. Finally, we looked at various ideas that can be loosely grouped under the heading of constructionism. We saw that some of these were quite close to interpretivism, at least in recommending the careful documentation of how particular social phenomena are culturally or interactionally constructed in particular places at particular times; though constructionism usually involves a different understanding of what this requires. We also noted more radical versions of this methodological philosophy that turn the notion of construction back on qualitative inquiry itself, implying that the accounts it produces can claim no more epistemic authority than any others. Here, at most, the role of such inquiry can only be to highlight the constructed, rather than 'natural' or 'scientific', character of dominant ways of thinking, and perhaps thereby to subvert them.

3 Divergent analytic styles

In the previous chapter I outlined some methodological philosophies that have shaped qualitative research, and that have been a major factor in generating the diverse forms it now takes. One consequence of this diversification has been a degree of terminological confusion: there is now a plethora of terms surrounding the practice of qualitative research, and the meaning of these is contextually variable and sometimes disputed. In particular, there are many words or phrases used either as near-synonyms for 'qualitative inquiry', or to identify sub-types of it, that do not form part of a well-formed typology; in other words, their relations with one another are uncertain. These terms include: 'ethnography', 'case study', 'naturalistic inquiry', 'field research', 'participant observation', 'interpretive study', 'phenomenological inquiry', 'hermeneutic investigation', 'ethnomethodology', 'narrative inquiry', 'discourse analysis', 'virtual ethnography', 'visual anthropology', 'linguistic ethnography', and others.[1]

In discussing different kinds of qualitative research, a commonly used contrast is between ethnography and discourse analysis. This can be helpful: it certainly signals an important difference in orientation. The term 'ethnography' generally refers to work that draws on a variety of data sources, with participant observation often treated as central. Thus, the ethnographer usually participates, overtly or covertly, in people's daily lives for an extended period of time, watching what happens, listening to what is said, and/or asking questions through informal and formal interviews, collecting documents and artifacts – indeed, gathering any available data that can illuminate the emerging focus of inquiry (Hammersley and Atkinson 2007). By contrast, discourse analysis tends to employ as data various types of text, whether documents of some kind, or transcriptions of audio-or video-recordings. It usually employs relatively small amounts

1 A useful source for clarification of the meanings of these and other terms associated with qualitative research is Schwandt (2001).

of data, compared to ethnography, and does not normally mix different kinds. Furthermore, it focuses specifically upon the functioning of particular textual features or patterns, these sometimes being analysed in relation to local or wider contexts.

Despite these differences, each of the two labels covers a heterogeneous field, involving very significant internal divergences in orientation (Hammersley 2005). Nor do they exhaust the range of work that comes under the heading of 'qualitative research'. So, instead, I will identify four relatively distinct sorts of focus that qualitative researchers have adopted: identifying causes; investigating experience; penetrating fronts; and documenting constitutive practices. These are ideal types identifying significant differences across the field of qualitative research, not just in terms of focus but also in underlying assumptions.[2]

Identifying causes

Causal analysis has often been regarded as central to science, and it was the focus of much discussion of scientific method in the nineteenth century. It is also central to most quantitative research today. Interestingly, though, some early advocates of qualitative method challenged the ability of 'statistical method' to identify causes, on the grounds that it can only produce probabilistic statements – whereas, they claimed, causal laws state what *always* happens when certain conditions hold. These writers argued that qualitative case study, by contrast, is uniquely capable of uncovering causal relations, for example through using 'analytic induction' (see Znaniecki 1934).

Today, under the influence of interpretivism and constructionism, many qualitative researchers would deny that they are engaged in causal analysis, or even that causal relations operate in the social world. One reason for this is that they often see the very notion of causality as denying human agency; and they regard agency as a central feature of social life, recognition of which is also an important ethical or political principle. In other words, they believe that to focus on how behaviour is socially determined dehumanizes human beings, portraying them as – indeed perhaps

2 For a similar typology, omitting the first type, see Grahame (1999). There are still kinds of work that this typology does not take into account. These include qualitative action research, such as that of Kaplan mentioned in Box 1.1, and also those forms of qualitative inquiry that have turned to 'socio-poetics', see Ellis and Bochner (1996).

inducing them to become – automatons or dopes. Furthermore, the concept of causality is sometimes taken to imply that there is no possibility of changing social arrangements for the better, and most qualitative researchers oppose this as political conservatism.

Another reason why qualitative researchers often reject the idea that causation operates in the social world is that this is taken to deny the complexity and contingency that they believe is characteristic of that world. However, this rejection is based on a very strong interpretation of the concept of causality; ironically, exactly the one that Znaniecki insisted upon. This assumes that universal laws can be discovered which state that one type of thing (X) is *always* followed by another (Y), and that what precedes a Y is *always* an X. However, there are weaker notions of causal relation, one of which claims only that an X *tends to be followed by* a Y, as a result of some force exerted by the occurrence of an X rather than by happenstance. This is the sense of the term 'cause' adopted by most quantitative research.

While many qualitative researchers now explicitly reject causal analysis, in practice most nevertheless engage in it, tending to assume the weaker notion of causation just outlined. This is signaled by the fact that they routinely use words like 'influence', 'shape', 'leads to', 'results in', etc. (Hammersley 2008b). Thus, much qualitative research displays an interest in what leads to or influences what, and/or in what are the consequences of particular practices or institutional arrangements. Referring back to the examples of qualitative research cited in Chapter 1, this is most obviously true of Wright and Decker's work on factors contributing to the occurrence of armed robbery and Olson *et al's* study of suicide notes, but in one way or another it applies to almost all the other examples as well.

If we look at discussions of qualitative methodology we can sometimes find acknowledgement that causal analysis is the aim. One example is the very influential account of 'grounded theorizing' put forward by Glaser and Strauss (see Dey 2007: 178–9), in which the aim is to build theories through an iterative process of collecting data, generating explanatory ideas, and developing them through the systematic selection of cases for subsequent investigation. Indeed, the focus of this kind of work on causal processes has been retained implicitly even in recent attempts to exorcise 'positivist' aspects of it in favour of a more constructionist approach (see Charmaz 2000, 2006: 9–10; Bryant and Charmaz 2007: 36–41 and 2011).

In the field of political science in recent years a strong case has been made for the value of qualitative case study as a means of causal analysis, though this time as a complement to quantitative work rather than (as in the case of Znaniecki) a replacement for it (see Mahoney and Goertz 2006). Case study, often historical in character, has long played an influential role in Western political science. While, in the second half of the twentieth century, it was marginalized by the development of sophisticated quantitative work, in the past decade or so there has been a sustained methodological defence of the capacity of qualitative case study to identify causes, and an increasing number of qualitative studies adopting this orientation (see, for instance, Bennett and Elman 2006).

Methods used

There is little or no restriction on the methods of data collection that can be used in qualitative research aimed at causal analysis. Early work in sociology that built on Znaniecki's analytic induction tended to rely upon interviews, though often supplemented by some participant observation and the use of documents (see Lindesmith 1937, 1968; Cressey 1953; Becker 1953, 1955, 1973). Studies employing grounded theorizing have also employed a wide range of qualitative data. Meanwhile, in political science, as already noted, the main kind of data has often been historical documents of one sort or another, or secondary textual sources.

In seeking to identify causes, qualitative research typically relies, to varying degrees, upon two forms of analysis. First there is in-depth study of particular cases seeking to 'trace' patterns of causation over time within them, both through observation by researchers and/or by drawing on the reports of participants. What are involved here are inferences about causes from data about sequences and patterns of events, participants' attitudes, etc, along the lines of Alasuutari's 'riddle-solving' (see Chapter 1). In many respects, this is similar to the work of historians seeking to explain key events (see Roberts 1996).

The second method, cross-case analysis, is concerned with similarities among cases where the outcome or process being studied occurred, and/or differences *between* these cases and those where it did not occur. Such comparisons can be used as a basis for developing, and then checking, inferences about likely causal relationships; in short, building explanations or theories. This is a strategy that is shared with quantitative research, but within qualitative work the concern is usually with careful comparison of a small number of cases rather than investigating associations across large samples or populations. Furthermore, there is often an interest in exploring the role of *combinations* of causal factors, rather than simply seeking to assess the causal contribution of each factor separately in the manner of most quantitative work. This 'configurational' approach is central to 'qualitative comparative analysis', which was first developed in the field of political science but is now being applied much more widely (Ragin 2000; Rihoux and Ragin 2009).

Criticisms

As already indicated, many qualitative researchers reject causal analysis for ethical and political reasons, and/or on the grounds that the social world is characterized by complex and contingent relations that are not causal in character, in the sense that they are very different from those operating in the physical world. There are also criticisms of qualitative causal analysis from the quantitative side. Here the main charges are that too few cases are studied for general conclusions to be reached, and that it involves inadequate control over variables, so that even findings about the cases investigated are unlikely to be reliable (King *et al.* 1994; Lieberson 1991 and 1994; but see also Brady and Collier 2004).

Investigating experience

In this second orientation, research is aimed at exploring in depth the experience and perspectives of some group or type of people, perhaps even just one person. Examples mentioned in Chapter 1 include Bogdan's life history of Jane Fry and Lewis's study of people's experiences of irritable bowel syndrome. This second orientation is often strongly influenced by interpretivism, including phenomenology.

A central assumption here is that people's experiences and perspectives are more diverse, complex and interesting than is generally recognized; and that documenting them is therefore intrinsically worthwhile, this point of view sometimes being labeled 'critical humanism' (see Plummer 2001). There is often a particular emphasis on the need to study the experiences and perspectives of people who are marginalized, ignored, or oppressed within a society, for example minority ethnic or religious groups, mental patients and prisoners, the poor and the homeless, gays and lesbians, etc. Indeed, sometimes the analytic task is seen as 'giving voice' to such people, or gaining voice oneself as such a person, as with much feminist research and queer theory. At the very least, a primary aim may be to overcome what is viewed as misrepresentation of these groups in official accounts, established theories, popular stereotypes, and current ideologies.

It is also sometimes argued that documenting people's experience and perspectives *in detail* is essential if we are to understand their actions. To take just one example, it has long been recognized that the behaviour of many patients, particularly older people, who have been prescribed drugs fails to conform with instructions about how these should be used. However, simply labeling them 'non-compliant with prescribed regimens' provides us with little insight, indeed it leads in the direction of blame and/or dismissal of their behaviour as irrational. Instead, it is argued, we need to investigate people's attitudes towards their medical condition, and towards themselves, and their views about the character and effectiveness of particular drugs and their side-effects. Unless we understand their perspectives on these matters, it is insisted, we will not be able to understand their behaviour.[3]

Investigating experience may, therefore, be prompted by, or lead to, a concern with *explaining* people's behaviour. This is often seen as a matter of documenting the *reasons* why they behave as they do – in other words the focus is on their intentions and expressed motives. Indeed, there is often an assumption that people are 'experts' on themselves, and that no purely external account in terms of situational adaptation or background factors can be adequate. It is argued that people have more information about themselves and what they do than any researcher could ever hope to gain, or it may be assumed that through self-analysis they are uniquely placed to grasp the complexity of the motivations behind their actions.

Generally speaking, those adopting this orientation assume that understanding other people's perspectives is a challenging task, not to be taken on lightly in either methodological or ethical terms, and one that is by no means assured of success. For example, in relation to life history work, the study of people's biographies, Plummer writes:

> In a way, I am simply advocating getting close to living human beings, accurately yet imaginatively picking up the way they express their understandings of the world around them, perhaps providing

3 See Pound *et al.* (2005) for a synthesis of findings from qualitative studies on this topic.

> an analysis of such expressions, presenting them in interesting ways, and being self-critically aware of the immense difficulties such tasks bring. (Plummer 2001: 2)

The difficulties involved take a variety of forms. For one thing, it is not always straightforward to get people to talk: they may not be interested in research, they may not understand why the researcher would be interested in what they have to say, or what they could say that would be of interest; they may fear that what they reveal will be embarrassing – putting themselves or others in a bad light – or damaging; and/or there may be secrets they do not wish to disclose.

Aside from this, researchers themselves must overcome the effects of, or at least try to suspend, many of their personal and cultural assumptions, and perhaps especially their routine attitudes and evaluations. This is necessary if they are to ask questions and make responses that encourage candid accounts of people's experiences and points of view. It is also crucial if they are to be able to *understand* these experiences and perspectives, so as to document them accurately and in detail. Very often this will require a process of learning – one that is informal in character and necessarily open-ended – in which the influence of the researcher's initial ideas must be minimized to prevent their operating as a source of blindness or bias.

We can illustrate the difficulties here by considering the case of adult researchers seeking to understand the experience and perspectives of children. It has been argued that this is a very difficult task because children are alien or 'other' in relation to adults: children operate at distinctive stages of psychological development, have not yet been fully socialized, and they have distinctive conditions of life. This means that in order to understand them adults must work hard to put aside what seems normal and obvious, and attempt to learn to see and feel things differently. And there are those who raise doubts about whether, or about the extent to which, this can ever be possible. For example, Jones (2001: 177) has argued:

> Once childhood is superseded by adult stocks of knowledge, those adult filters can never be removed to get back to earlier states. Adult constructions and memories of what it is/was to be a child are inevitably processed through adultness.

Similar arguments can be found in other cases – men in relation to women, or people from one social class, culture, or generation seeking to understand those from others. Indeed, here the problem could be even more challenging than in the case of understanding children, since all adults have at some time actually *been* children.

Of course, while researchers will always differ in some respects from the people they study, there will usually be much that they also share. This suggests that there is normally at least some scope for learning to understand others' perspectives, even if there are also barriers that create potential misunderstandings. Equally important is the other side of this point: that even when a researcher shares a key identity with the people being studied, understanding cannot be guaranteed, since there will always be other ways in which he or she differs from them. For example, Reinharz (1997), in her research on elderly kibbutzim members in Israel, came to realize both the value of being an Ashkenazi Jew, like the people she was studying, but also the significance of her differences from them, especially the fact that she was only a temporary member of the kibbutz.

Methods used

Researchers adopting this second orientation frequently rely primarily upon in-depth interviews as the best means of eliciting accounts of people's experience and perspectives. These interviews will generally be relatively unstructured in character, and often carried out in contexts where interviewees feel relaxed, with the aim of allowing them to speak at length in their own terms. As part of this, the interviewer will often engage in considerable efforts to build and sustain rapport, while at the same time trying to minimize her or his influence. Of course, it may be necessary for the interviewer to intervene to stimulate people to talk about topics that they have glossed over, or to prompt them to provide more detail about examples that they have only mentioned, but this will usually be done in ways that go along with the flow of what the informant is saying rather than disrupting it. In short, the usual interviewing style adopted is responsive in character, aiming to facilitate the elicitation of data relevant to understanding people's experiences and perspectives. This sort of approach is characteristic, for example, of the kinds of interview used in much life-history and biographical work.[4]

Within this orientation, interviews may sometimes be supplemented by observation of people in the contexts that they normally inhabit, on the grounds that this can facilitate the researcher's understanding of what they believe and why, as well as of what they do. For example, in their study of first-time mothers, Thomson *et al.* (2011) combined repeated interviews with 'day in the life' observations.

Of course, there are occasions when neither interview nor observation will be possible, and here reliance may be placed entirely upon documents. Indeed, it may be argued that what is provided through the written word is superior in some respects, for instance because it involves more forethought and careful formulation. Various kinds of documents can be used through which the researcher attempts to understand people's beliefs and actions. These include, most obviously, personal diaries or blogs, but there are other kinds too. As we saw in Chapter 1, in their study of suicide Olson *et al.* (2011) used suicide notes; and in her study of friendship among teenage girls in school Valerie Hey (1997) made considerable use of the notes that they passed to one another in lessons. Researchers may also *elicit* documents, for example by asking people to keep diaries or to take photographs or make videos of significant places or events in their lives. In his research on irritable bowel syndrome, cited in Chapter 1, Lewis (2006) used an open-ended on-line questionnaire to gain information about people's experiences.

As we have seen, it is often recognized that any understanding that researchers obtain of others' perspectives will necessarily be filtered through their own distinctive view of the world, their attitudes, feelings, and so on; though it might reasonably be argued that these are not simply a source of potential blindness or bias but are also essential in facilitating understanding. Nevertheless, it follows from this that what is produced reflects a transaction between the two perspectives, rather than a simple representation by researchers of other people's viewpoints and experiences. This often motivates a requirement that the researcher explicate her or his own perspective before providing an account of the perspectives of others, so that readers of research reports can understand the

4 See, for example, the Timescapes projects (accessed 24.4.12): http://www.timescapes.leeds.ac.uk/research-projects/

interplay between the two (although, of course, readers' understandings of this interplay will, in turn, be filtered through their own perspectives). Some have pressed this requirement for 'reflexivity' further, for example coming to argue that autoethnography (see Ellis 2004) is superior to studying others directly, given that no-one can get beyond her or his own experience.[5]

Criticisms

This second orientation has by no means escaped criticism. Aside from doubts about the very possibility of understanding others' experience and perspectives, there have also been arguments that it relies upon a defective psychology. The charge is that it fails to recognize that inner experience is always socio-culturally constituted; for instance, that the kinds of talk elicited through in-depth interviews about people's experiences will reflect the particular genres concerned with thoughts, feelings, etc. that are available within the culture concerned, and how these have been mobilized on the particular occasion – rather than simply displaying individual forms of inner experience and belief in themselves. Moreover, these genres will differ across societies and social groups. Also challenged sometimes is the idea that people truly understand themselves and their behaviour. Drawing on Marxism or psychoanalysis, for example, it may be argued that there are psychological or social forces that lead people systematically to misunderstand themselves and their world.

In addition, there are some ethical and political arguments against this orientation. Most obviously, it may be seen as invading privacy, and there are associated arguments that it reflects the prevalence of an individualizing discourse through which people's very selves are opened up to public surveillance; or that it transforms what should be public issues into a preoccupation with personalities (see Atkinson and Silverman 1997; Gubrium and Holstein 2001; Bauman 2000).

Penetrating fronts

The third orientation or style I will discuss is concerned with finding out *what actually happens* in some situation as against what official accounts

5 For an important debate about autoethnography, see the *Journal of Contemporary Ethnography*, Vol 35, Issue 4, August 2006.

say happens, or discovering what people *actually* do rather than what they say they do, or documenting what they *really* believe or feel as against what they claim to believe or feel. Mitchell's (2001) study of 'survivalists', outlined in Box 1.1 provides an example of this sort of approach. Underlying it is the idea that people, groups, and organizations put up 'fronts', whether consciously or unconsciously, whether routinely or on particular occasions, and whether for the protection of themselves and others or to promote sectional interests (Goffman 1959; Douglas 1976). Whatever the motive, it is assumed that these fronts obscure or misrepresent people's real intentions, attitudes, beliefs, goals, and practices, so that the task of the researcher is to get behind them to discover the truth.

This is clearly very different from the second orientation, which treats people as reliable experts on themselves and their own behaviour. Instead, what seems to be required here is what has been referred to as a 'hermeneutics of suspicion' (Gadamer 1984; Leiter 2005); in which the 'principle of charity', whereby we assume that people are honest and know what they claim to know, is suspended.

It is sometimes argued that the creation of fronts is especially common among those in powerful positions, and that it is the responsibility of social scientists to investigate the attitudes and actions of such people and publicize what they find – in the interests of openness, accountability and democracy. In other words, this orientation may be seen as performing an important political function, analogous to that of the investigative journalist (Rainwater and Pittman 1967; Christie 1976; Douglas 1976; Lundman and McFarlane 1976). In some respects, this focus is influenced by the 'critical' methodological philosophy we discussed in the previous chapter, but it is not restricted to that tradition. At the very least, what is assumed is that society is characterized by conflicting interests and endemic deception, at least in certain quarters.

Of course, research aimed at penetrating fronts need not be directed at the most powerful groups in a society. It can be argued that most of us use fronts of one sort or another, so that there are many areas of life where what really goes on is not publicly known, even when it is widely suspected. Examples that have been researched include what goes on in massage parlours (Douglas 1976), what happens in gay bath houses (Styles 1979), and the services (including the supply of drugs) provided by some 'bouncers' on the doors of night clubs (Calvey 2000).

Methods used

Researchers employing this orientation often stress the importance of carrying out observations in natural settings, going to 'where the action is' often 'behind closed doors', and studying everyday behaviour that is unaffected, or only minimally affected, by the research process. As in the case of Douglas's and Calvey's work, this may frequently involve the use of covert strategies: taking on some role in order to get access to a setting secretly, or infiltrating a scene by 'passing' as a member. After all, it is unlikely that people will agree to give access to a researcher who they know is going to expose what is really happening, and thereby undercut their carefully constructed and assiduously maintained fronts.

Interviews may also be used, either as the main source of data or as an important supplement to observation. They can supply evidence about the fronts to be penetrated, but also perhaps provide access to inside information about what goes on behind them. While in this latter role interviews are sometimes treated as second-best to direct observation, in many cases they will be the only source of data available. It is often argued that the selection of informants is crucial here: that it is necessary to target those who both know 'what really goes on' *and* have a motive for revealing it. This might include, for instance, people central to a group or organization who bear a grudge against others within it, those who are in subordinate positions but who witness key decisions (such as advisers or secretaries), and old-timers who may feel they have little to lose; as well as people who have recently left the group or organization, who may feel freer and more motivated to talk about what goes on within it – though like the others they may have axes to grind.

Interviews in this kind of research will often be rather different in character from those used for 'investigating experience'. While gaining inside information may require the researcher to build trust with interviewees, and to provide a context in which they can relax, at other times interview tactics will need to be challenging and even aggressive – aimed at forcing people to 'come clean', to face up to contradictions and explain themselves fully rather than offering superficial justifications or making excuses (see Douglas 1976).

Research concerned with 'penetrating fronts' may also sometimes use documents. These can certainly provide data about official accounts, but they can also sometimes be used to get behind these to find out what really goes on, especially when they have been produced for private purposes. Internal memos or emails, secret files, etc., generated within organizations for internal consumption may become available as a consequence of legal prosecution or unofficial leaks. And they may well contradict the official line presented in publicly available documents, where the aim is usually to portray the organization in the best public light and to promote its interests. However, even official documents intended for publication can sometimes be inadvertently revealing.

In the case of individuals, private diaries or letters may of course display much more about their actual attitudes and behaviour than what they say in more public forums. An example, from within qualitative research itself, is provided by the founding father of modern anthropology, Bronislaw Malinowski (1884–1942), whose published account of field-work practice highlighted the need for sympathetic understanding of 'the native point of view'. This account was taken as a kind of mission statement by many anthropologists. However, after his death, his personal diaries dating from the time of his first piece of fieldwork were published, and these revealed rather unsympathetic, perhaps even racist, attitudes towards the people he was studying (see Malinowski, 1967; Wax, 1972).

Criticisms

The commitment to penetrating fronts is probably less common among qualitative researchers in most fields today than it was in the past, though it has by no means entirely disappeared. The decline probably reflects concerns about the ethics of this kind of work, these no doubt compounded by the rise of ethical regulation (see Hammersley and Traianou 2012: ch.1). It may also stem from uncertainty about whether research can ever 'get behind' appearances to what 'actually occurred' or to what people 'truly believe'. Indeed, as we saw in Chapter 2, there can be doubts – fuelled by constructionism – about whether these phrases have any meaning at all.

Documenting constitutive practices

This fourth orientation within qualitative research is strongly influenced by constructionism, of one sort or another. Here, the focus is on the constitutive practices that generate social phenomena. These practices can be conceptualized in a variety of ways. While, most commonly, they relate to discourse, there has also been much research of this kind concerned with images, from early work on semiotics to more recent 'visual' anthropology or sociology (Ball and Smith 1992; Bignell 1997; Banks 2001; Pink 2007). Furthermore, some researchers argue that the whole of human behaviour is designed to be 'accountable' in the sense of being intelligible to others (Garfinkel 1967; Heritage 1984). Examples of this fourth orientation cited in Chapter 1 would be the studies by MacLure and Walker, Wetherell and Edley, and Levitas, all of them focusing on discourse, but employing rather different strategies and types of data from one another.

Central to much discourse analysis, as noted earlier, is the argument that linguistic accounts do not simply re-present the objects to which they refer but rather *constitute* those objects. In addition, some discourse analysts emphasize that language-use is not simply a means of communication, it is a medium through which actions and activities are performed. Thus, discursive strategies are always aimed at particular audiences, and are usually designed to produce particular effects. Equally important, it is emphasized that discursive strategies can lead us to believe things without question: to 'see' the world as having some essential character, ruling out other possibilities as effectively unthinkable. For this reason, some approaches under this heading, notably those influenced by the work of Foucault, emphasise the close relationship between discourse and the exercise of power.

The emergence of this kind of approach can be illustrated by a significant change that has taken place amongst sociologists studying the family. For most of the twentieth century, the focus in this field was typically on how and why family structures have changed over the course of Western history, for example from predominantly extended family forms to nuclear families, on how such structures vary across different types of society, and on the implications of this for gender roles, care of children, etc. However, many sociologists now focus instead on 'family practices' (Morgan 1996, 2011a and b), this term referring to the various kinds of activity through which people seek to establish and maintain what they see as their family, or at least some form of family life. In some cases, this has resulted in a preoccupation with how 'family' is constituted in and through the discursive practices in which people engage, including in research interviews (see Gubrium and Holstein 1990). For example, Gubrium and Holstein (1993: 663) declare that: 'Family is enacted wherever it is talked about, described, challenged, praised, or explicitly dismissed.' Another focus has been on the role of artifacts, such as photographs, used to display 'family' (Finch 2007).

With this fourth orientation, then, researchers are interested in how the accounts that people give (whether in interviews, in ordinary talk, in documents, or visually through photographs) are constructed, thereby representing the world in one way rather than another, and/or on how they function to bring off, or bring about, particular forms of action or institutional pattern. One aspect of this is exploring how stories are structured and the way that this shapes how they are read. Such *narrative analysis* draws many of its techniques from earlier investigations of imaginative literature, and the capacity of this to create believable worlds (Atkinson 1997; Andrews *et al.* 2000; Atkinson and Delamont 2004; Riessman 2008). A major focus has been on the narratives that people construct about themselves, and how these formulate their identities in some ways rather than others.

There is also discourse analysis concerned with conversational and other kinds of social interaction, focusing on the discursive resources and strategies employed (ten Have 2004 and 2007). Here, very often, it is argued that particular practices *generate their own contexts*. In other words, these strategies are seen as reflexively constituting the world in which they occur. In line with this, there is sometimes an insistence that there must be minimal reliance by the analyst, and by readers, upon any information about external 'context': it is insisted that what is relevant to understanding any piece of discourse is restricted to what is actually displayed as contextually relevant *in the data*.

By contrast, other research on discursive practices seeks to locate these within a context defined by the researcher, either through some theoretical account of the nature of the wider society or via evidence from other kinds of research. An example of this kind of work would be critical discourse analysis (Caldas-Coulthard and Coulthard 1996; Fairclough 2003). Here it is argued, for example, that if we are to understand why members of ethnic minorities are described in negative ways in tabloid newspapers then we need to understand the ideological roles that such minorities play within capitalist societies, as well as studying the discursive strategies employed by the mass media and the social functions they perform (van Dijk 1991).

So, research following this fourth orientation can range from studies of how stories are told or how particular kinds of social interaction are collaboratively realized, through to investigations of how textual strategies in the media reproduce capitalism or racism, or Foucault-inspired analysis of the discourses operating in particular institutional fields within particular historical periods.

Methods used

Given the diverse range of work and ideas included under this heading, it is perhaps not surprising that there are conflicting views about what sort of data should be employed. Fieldnotes produced by the researcher are generally ruled out by discourse analysts, of whatever stripe, because they depend so heavily upon what the researcher has looked out for, noticed and recorded. Instead, it is usually argued that observational data must be recorded electronically, in audio- or video-form, and then transcribed, perhaps in such a way as to capture not just the words but the details of language-use – such as hesitation, repetition, overlap, pauses, and non-verbal contributions. Some of those engaging in this kind of work also reject the use of data from research interviews: because what informants say in those contexts is heavily shaped by the researcher. They insist, instead, on the exclusive use of 'naturally occurring' talk, or of available documents of one kind or another.

So, those adopting this orientation are interested in studying interactional, discursive, narrative, representational, or communicative strategies or processes. By comparison with the third orientation ('penetrating fronts'), it could be said that much of the research under this fourth heading is exclusively interested in how fronts are constructed and maintained. The important difference, however, is that, generally speaking, this fourth orientation does not assume – indeed, it may specifically deny – that there is any 'reality' behind the fronts to be disguised or obscured. Many discourse analysts (critical discourse analysis is an exception here) insist that there are simply different versions of the world produced through discursive strategies – all that there can be behind a front, from this point of view, are the practices that generated it.

Sometimes, in this kind of work, there is a reluctance to ascribe motives to those employing the discursive strategies documented, or to see these strategies as being consciously selected and deployed by human beings. Instead, the focus is solely on the strategies and how they function. After all, to ascribe motives would require researchers engaging in reality-construction themselves, rather than simply describing the processes, procedures or strategies through which particular social realities are created and sustained, particular activities 'brought off', or particular forms of life constituted. It would also assume the operation of agency on the part of those using the strategies, and this is challenged by some, notably those influenced by post-structuralism.

Criticisms

This fourth approach has also been subjected to considerable criticism. To one degree or another, it amounts to a major re-specification, indeed a transformation, of the focus of social research – in effect, ruling out many topics and methods as inappropriate, including those that are central to the first three orientations we have discussed.[6] There has often been criticism of work concerned with the details of particular discursive practices, such as conversation analysis, on the grounds that it is trivial and pointless; in other words, that it does not address issues that have social and political significance. By contrast, those approaches that seek to locate discursive practices within a wider analytic context supplied by the researcher have often been challenged for the speculative character of the framework they deploy. Finally, it may be argued that these kinds of work rely upon constructionism but do not recognize its radical implications for any treatment of material as 'data', or for any claim to have documented practices operating in the world (Ashmore and Reed 2000; Ashmore *et al.* 2004).

Relationships among the four orientations

To varying degrees, and in different ways, these four styles of qualitative work offer a sharp contrast with quantitative research, with its aim of producing reliable measurement of manipulated variables from which widely generalizable conclusions can be derived through hypothesis-testing. At the same time, it is not hard to see that the four orientations are also in conflict with one another in important respects.

The first orientation, 'identifying causes', is perhaps the closest to quantitative research: it is concerned with the same sort of task – developing and testing explanatory hypotheses – even if it approaches this in a

6 It is sometimes argued that discourse and narrative analysis can be applied to any social topic, but this is disingenuous since the application transforms the topic, as normally understood, into one that is amenable to this form of analysis.

different way. It displays minimal signs of the influence of interpretivism, and virtually none of constructionism, though it is compatible with some versions of 'critical' philosophy, and with a commitment to penetrating fronts; and it does not rule out an interest in explaining the perspectives of individual actors.

The second orientation, 'investigating experience', treats what people say as a window into distinctive personal or cultural worlds, ones that, it is assumed, will make sense in their own terms. By contrast, the third approach, 'penetrating fronts', adopts a more critical attitude: the researcher is concerned with the reality behind the fronts that people present, which may only be detectable by ignoring what they say, or at least treating it with great suspicion, and observing what they *actually do* or what they say in unguarded moments. Whereas the second orientation requires the researcher to accept individuals' own accounts on trust, even where these do not initially make much sense, in the expectation that it is in principle possible to understand them, the prevailing stance in this third orientation is to be suspicious of what people say even if it apparently makes good sense, since it may simply be highly effective rationalization.

The fourth approach, 'documenting constitutive practices', is, in its purer forms, significantly at odds with all the others. It may deny both the existence of causal relations and the possibility of accessing the 'subjective realities' of other people – how they truly see and feel about the world – as well as denying that these are the well-springs of their actions. It may also question the existence of any objective reality behind the 'fronts' that people put up. Instead, the focus is primarily upon how social phenomena are constituted in and through various practices, the use of particular cultural resources, and so on.

Despite the tensions among the four orientations, many qualitative researchers in fact draw on several of them, though one or other is usually given primary emphasis. As we saw, the second may be used to discover causal processes, and the focus on what goes on behind fronts may also be concerned with this. The second and third may be combined, sometimes even in the same study, one being applied to those people with whom the researcher has some sympathy, political or personal, the other to those with whom he or she has none (see Hammersley 1998). There is also a tendency for researchers to apply the fourth orientation to accounts that they assume to be spurious, on the (mistaken) assumption that because an account can be shown to be a construction it must therefore be false.

Furthermore, as we noted, there are less pure forms of discourse analysis and semiotic analysis that seek to locate the study of constitutive practices within broader accounts of the world, which might be supplied by research carried out under one or more of the other orientations.

In the next chapter we will look at a couple of controversies among qualitative researchers that have specifically revolved around tensions between these approaches, and the methodological philosophies that underpin them.

4 Two methodological disputes

It will perhaps come as no surprise, given the substantial differences in philosophical assumption and practical orientation to be found amongst social researchers today, that there have been, and continue to be, major methodological and theoretical disputes. Moreover, these have occurred not just across the qualitative-quantitative divide but also very frequently *among* different versions of qualitative research. At the most fundamental level, these disputes relate to what sorts of knowledge are possible and desirable, and to the nature and goal of the research enterprise. It is not possible to cover all of the issues that divide qualitative researchers, but I will focus on two very different disputes each of which raises important and difficult methodological problems. Discussion of these is designed to give a sense of the variations in underlying commitment that generate much of the diversity, in both rhetoric and practice, now to be found in qualitative research.

The first dispute centres on the legitimacy of employing interviews as a source of data, though as we shall see its implications extend much more widely – to the use of observational data and documents as well. The second dispute focuses on recent ethnographic work concerned with the lives of the urban poor in the United States, raising challenging questions about the role of theory and evidence, and about the public or political responsibility of researchers.

The 'radical critique' of interviews

Interviews have long been used by qualitative researchers as a central source of data, and in fact studies relying primarily or entirely on this type of data have become increasingly common in recent decades; a trend that has attracted criticism (see, for example, Atkinson and Silverman 1997; Silverman 2007: ch.2). In Chapter 3 we saw that interviews are often central to research that is concerned with investigating people's experience and perspectives, and that they may also play an important role in work aimed at identifying causal relations or penetrating fronts, and even in some research that seeks to document discursive practices.

Qualitative researchers have generally adopted a very different approach to interviewing from survey researchers. They have used informal as well as formal (in other words, pre-arranged) interviews, and their aim, generally speaking, has been to encourage informants to talk in their own terms about matters relevant to the research topic. In other words, they have tended to use a relatively unstructured approach. As part of this, the aim has *usually* been to minimize the impact of the interviewer on what the informant says (this impact sometimes being referred to as 'reactivity'). In addition, stress is placed upon the importance of listening, on the researcher trying to suspend her or his preconceptions and prejudices in order to understand the perspectives, feelings, or accounts of informants.

Despite these distinctive features, much qualitative analysis uses interviews for more or less the same purposes as other kinds of social science:

1. *As a source of witness information about the social world.* Here, interviews are treated as supplying information about informants' biographies, about events they have observed, about relevant stable or variable features of situations they are familiar with, and/or about the frequency of one or more types of event in such situations.
2. *As a source of participant-analysis.* Here, interviewees are asked to reflect upon their own behaviour, attitudes, character, and/or personality, and perhaps also on that of other people they know, so as to supply their own interpretations. These are then used by the researcher – subject to critical assessment.
3. *As an indirect source of evidence about informants' attitudes or perspectives.* Here, the analyst uses how informants respond to questions as a basis for drawing inferences about their characteristic intentions, motives, preoccupations, preferences, perspectives, attitudes, etc. It is frequently assumed that what can be detected here are stable orientations that generate behaviour beyond the interview setting, though perhaps in a contextually variable manner. And the responses of informants may be treated as typical of some general category of person, or of a larger population.

Much analysis of interview data in qualitative research is directed at all three of these purposes, to varying degrees; and it is not always easy to distinguish between them in practice, even though they are analytically distinct.

There have long been discussions among qualitative researchers about the value and use of interview data, raising questions for example about whether and how we can 'know the informant is telling the truth' (Dean and Whyte 1958), about the 'incompleteness' of interview data as compared with that from participant observation (Becker and Geer 1957), and about the difference between what people say and what they do (Deutscher 1973). However, the more recent 'radical critique' of interviews takes a skeptical, constructionist line that is at odds not only with much current practice but also with these earlier criticisms (Murphy *et al.* 1998). In effect, the radical critique rejects the use of interview data as a window on the world and/or into the minds of informants (Dingwall 1997; Silverman 1997; Atkinson and Coffey 2002).

As an example of this critique, I will focus on an article by Potter and Hepburn (2005) entitled 'Qualitative interviews in psychology: problems and possibilities.' This article was accompanied by three commentaries in the same journal issue, to which Potter and Hepburn then replied. In their initial article the authors outline their aim as 'to challenge the taken-for-granted position of the open-ended interview as the method of choice in modern qualitative psychology' (Potter and Hepburn 2005: 282). They criticize, in particular, the way in which interview data are usually reported and interpreted, but what they say also has implications for when, if ever, interviews should be used.[1]

Potter and Hepburn distinguish between problems that are remediable ('contingent'), and others that they suggest may be inherent in the use of interviews ('necessary'). Under the first heading they list the following:

1. The interviewer is typically viewed by researchers as simply eliciting pre-existing attitudes, perspectives, etc, possessed by the informant, and as a result her or his role is given little attention in the analysis. Equally important, information about questions asked is rarely included in the transcript excerpts published in research reports. The effect of this, Potter and Hepburn suggest, is to treat what informants say as if they were offering abstract pronouncements about matters

1 While their article is concerned with qualitative methods in psychology, their arguments apply across social science. For a similar critique relating to qualitative research more generally, see Rapley (2001).

rather than giving 'a specific answer to a specific question put by a specific interviewer' (Potter and Hepburn 2005: 286).

2. There is a failure to attend to other aspects of the *interactional* character of interviews. Potter and Hepburn argue that the forms of transcription generally used by qualitative researchers systematically strip out much that is relevant, for example hesitations, overlaps, the timing of pauses, emphasis, etc.[2] Equally important, research reports quote very short extracts from transcripts that give little sense of surrounding context.
3. Because they use transcripts that omit interactional detail, when analyzing their data most qualitative researchers fail to relate their claims to specific features, making 'global' statements whose validity is difficult to assess.
4. There is often little information provided about the set-up of the interview. Yet, how it was arranged, not least what interviewees were told about the research, and about why they were being invited to participate, could have shaped the data in important ways. As a result, readers may have difficulty assessing the validity of the evidence accurately.

A central complaint here, then, concerns the forms of transcription used by qualitative researchers and how these affect both the analysis carried out and the evidence made available to readers. On the basis of these complaints, Potter and Hepburn lay down four requirements:

i) Transcript extracts in research reports should include the relevant interview questions.
ii) These extracts should be 'transcribed to a level that allows interactional features to be appreciated even if interactional features are not the topic of the study' (Potter and Hepburn 2005: 291).
iii) Transcripts should be presented using line numbers, and short lines, to allow specific references to features within them.
iv) Research reports 'should include information about how participants were approached, under what categories, with what interview tasks' (Potter and Hepburn 2005: 291).

---

2 For an example of specific advice to *exclude* such features, see Finnegan (1992: 196–7) (quoted in Plummer 2001: 150).

The other type of problem that Potter and Hepburn identify in qualitative researchers' use of interview data, which they regard as intrinsic and unavoidable, includes the following:

1 Interviews tend to be 'flooded' by social science agendas and categories. This is not just a matter of research questions being explicitly mentioned to informants, or technical social science terms included in interview questions, but also of the more inexplicit ways in which the assumptions characteristic of a particular discipline may infuse the orientation of the researcher and affect the informant. These assumptions might include the idea that the social world is characterized by the operation of causal variables, or that people necessarily know about their own attitudes and behaviour (Potter and Hepburn 2005: 291). The suggestion is that through their questions, and in other ways, interviewers effectively 'coach [..] the participant in the relevant social science agenda' (Potter and Hepburn 2005: 292), and thereby subtly shape what he or she says. Potter and Hepburn summarise this concern as follows: '[...] these issues present us with the possibility that a piece of interview research is chasing its own tail, offering up its own agendas and categories, and getting those same agendas and categories back in a refined or filtered or inverted form' (Potter and Hepburn 2005: 293).
2 Rather than participants in interviews simply speaking for themselves, in fact what we find is that they echo other voices, speak on behalf of others, and so on. This is captured, in part, by the distinctions drawn by Goffman (1981) among various 'footings' that can be adopted in talk: for instance between the speaker and the composer of the spoken talk – as illustrated by a politician reading a speech written by someone else – and between the speaker and the 'voice' being represented – as when a spokesperson speaks on behalf of a government or other organization. Potter and Hepburn argue that analysts must attend to the different 'footings' people adopt in interviews, and they raise questions about the possibility of abstracting from these in order to make claims about people's general 'attitudes' or 'perspectives', as if they always or primarily spoke with single voices. More generally, while people are usually interviewed by researchers precisely because they are members of some category – teachers, social workers, politicians, etc – it is clear that not all of

what they say is spoken under the auspices of this particular identity. People always operate with a multiplicity of potentially relevant identities, and these are more or less salient at different times, even within the course of the same piece of social interaction. There is also the reverse question of to whom informants are talking: it cannot be assumed that their primary or only audience is the interviewer, since they will probably anticipate that others are likely to hear what they say, even if only via the research report. Moreover, even if we take the interviewer as the audience, he or she will have multiple identities, and may be oriented to by informants in terms of different ones at different times within the same interview.

3 When people talk, what they say is attuned to the stakes they have in how they might be interpreted, and the potential consequences of this. They are not, therefore, simply expressing their views, but seeking to 'position' themselves in response to anticipations of how they might be 'positioned' by others. Indeed, it is unclear whether, aside from this, they have some single position which underpins what they say. The implication of the argument here is that once we abandon the assumption that what is said is the simple expression of inner, personal thoughts or feelings, we can do no more than document the different 'attitudes' displayed on particular occasions by speakers and seek to understand these displays.

So, what conclusion should be drawn from this critique? On the face of it, the authors hedge their bets, offering two slightly different ones. They write that their 'ultimate aim is to improve the quality of interviews and their targeting at particular research problems. The ideal would be much less interview research, but much better interview research' (Potter and Hepburn 2005: 282). The implication here is that the findings from studying interviews as interactional processes can be fed back to improve the 'design, conduct and analysis of interviews so that [these] can be used more effectively in cases where [they] are the most appropriate data-gathering tools' (Potter and Hepburn 2005: 281). Along these lines, the authors argue that 'whatever the analytic perspective, inferring things appropriately from interviews involves understanding what is going on in them interactionally, and that in turn involves the complex and demanding task of analyzing the development of an implicit research agenda, identifying footing shifts, explicating orientations to stake and so on' (Potter and Hepburn 2005: 300).

However, Potter and Hepburn also comment that: 'As researchers with some expertise in interaction analysis we would like to emphasise that this is a challenging analytic requirement. Such analysis is rarely done with any degree of seriousness in current interview research, and, where it is, the analysis often highlights just how much the interviewee's talk is a product of specific features of the interview.' (Potter and Hepburn 2005: 300). This points to a second, rather different, conclusion: that interviews are not a satisfactory source of data, that it would be better to use 'naturally occurring data' (Potter and Hepburn 2005: 301).[3]

It is striking that, even in the case of this second more radical conclusion, Potter and Hepburn seem to imply that it derives from methodological considerations that would apply to all kinds of research, rather than specifically from 'a conversational analytic and discursive psychological perspective' (Potter and Hepburn 2005: 291).[4] Indeed, this point about general relevance is one that they make at various times in their article. Early on they comment that 'we expect researchers who work with interviews to recognize [the problems we are going to discuss] without difficulty' (Potter and Hepburn 2005: 282); and suggest that the points they are making 'are intended to have a much broader relevance than specifically to those researchers with a discourse or conversational interest' (Potter and Hepburn 2005: 282).

Yet, even their discussion of the problems they see as remediable is governed by distinctive assumptions about the nature of the social world, and how we can gain sound knowledge of it, that derive from an ethnomethodological or conversation analytic point of view. While other researchers would not deny that answers are shaped by the questions asked, even in relatively unstructured interviews, and that what is said there is influenced by other aspects of the interactional process, many are likely to regard the dangers as much less serious a potential source of error than Potter and Hepburn claim. Similarly, while most would agree that

3 As Potter and Hepburn acknowledge (2005: 301), there has been some debate about the possibility of 'naturalistic' data, and about whether it is essential for the kind of work they propose: see Speer (2002), Potter (2002), ten Have (2002), Speer and Hutchby (2003), Hammersley (2003).

4 Coulter (1999) has questioned the link between ethnomethodology and discursive psychology, see also Potter and Edwards (2003), and Coulter (2004).

analytic interpretations should be tied to evidence in research reports, there are differences in view about exactly what this entails.

Much the same can be said of the problems that the authors view as unavoidable. In fact, there was a fourth such problem they identified, which I have not yet mentioned, and this demonstrates the point particularly clearly. They call this fourth issue 'the reproduction of cognitivism'. There is some ambiguity in what they say here. They reject 'cognitivism', while at the same time recognising that: 'For many interview researchers some kind of cognitive perspective will be entirely appropriate.' (Potter and Hepburn 2005: 297). In fact, their arguments are at odds with the orientation of most qualitative researchers, and indeed even with that of many other discourse analysts.

Potter and Hepburn identify two 'facets' of cognitivism that are to be rejected: 'the privileging of rumination over action and the treatment of cognitive language as descriptive'. What becomes clear here is that Potter and Hepburn are, in effect, denying that interview data can be used for any of the three standard purposes I outlined earlier. As regards the first, they complain that in much qualitative work the interviewee is treated 'as a reporter on events, actions, social processes and structures, and cognitions' (Potter and Hepburn 2005: 298), whereas, in fact, informants are engaged in a quite different mode of activity, which might be described as constructing and reconstructing themselves and their world through talk.

In relation to the second function of interviews, Potter and Hepburn explicitly abandon the idea of using people's own 'rumination[s]' (Potter and Hepburn 2005: 297) as a source of data. In part this stems from their denial that people have privileged access to an inner domain of experience that they express through talk, since they must use *common* discursive resources to present *situationally appropriate* accounts of themselves. Indeed, Potter and Hepburn denounce the idea, taken for granted in much research concerned with investigating experience, that 'people are the best experts' (Potter and Hepburn 2005: 299) on their own perceptions, opinions, beliefs, attitudes, etc. Equally, it is clear that they object to researchers accepting people's explanations for what happens in the world, where they are, in effect, treated as 'proto-social scientists' (Potter and Hepburn 2005: 297). Potter and Hepburn 'highlight', by which (it seems to me) they mean 'challenge', the assumption that interviewees can provide information about social processes (Potter and Hepburn 2005: 298).

Finally, they reject the use of interviews as a means by which attitudes, perspectives, etc. can be identified because they deny that actions are causal products of such attitudes or perspectives. As we have seen, they question the existence of all such 'cognitive objects'. Thus, they write:

> Our point is that to fully understand the qualitative interview as an interaction we will need to pay attention to the practical and interactional role of cognitive terms and be very cautious about treating such terms as if they referred to psychological objects of some kind within individuals. (Potter and Hepburn 2005: 299)

Again, read in the context of the whole article, it is clear that 'caution' is a euphemism here, what they mean is that we should *not* treat these terms as referring to psychological objects.

So, in this section on cognitivism, Potter and Hepburn continue to present their arguments as if they derived straightforwardly from commonly recognisable methodological problems with interviews, but in effect they are challenging fundamental assumptions underlying much qualitative research. While they claim that their conclusions derive simply from recognising the interactional nature of interviews, in fact the character and seriousness of these problems have been and continue to be subject to conflicting implications and debate.[5] In other words, there is disagreement among social researchers about how much of an obstacle these problems represent. Moreover, presumably they are problems that face all of us in our everyday lives when we are interpreting evidence and constructing explanations about other people's behaviour; so does this mean that here too we must avoid reliance upon testimony from others? The answer is, presumably, no. At issue, then, is the difference between research and other activities, in terms of the evidential requirements they entail. Interestingly,

5 Most qualitative researchers are concerned with reactivity and how this might distort their findings, but they do not usually believe that because interviews involve interactional processes it is impossible to draw conclusions from them about the experiences and perspectives of informants, and about the world in which they live. For example, they do not assume that what an informant says in answer to a question is entirely determined by the nature of the question. Nor do they believe that because informants must use a particular natural language, and available discursive resources, that what they say is entirely determined by these resources. See the thoughtful discussion in Murphy and Dingwall (2003: ch.5) of 'what kind of information can we get from interview data?', illustrated by examples from the health field.

this is a contested matter even within the ethnomethodological tradition on which Potter and Hepburn draw (see Lynch 1993).

Finally we should note that the radical implications of the kind of constructionism that Potter and Hepburn adopt extend well beyond the use of interviews. In practice, these apply to all forms of data, whether audio-recordings of naturally occurring social interaction, textual documents, or visual images. For instance, when studying naturally occurring talk, discourse analysts (of the kind represented by Potter and Hepburn) do not use the data to draw conclusions about the experiences or perspectives of the people involved in the interaction, to show what is actually going on as against what is said to happen, or to identify causal relationships. Rather, they focus upon what they see as the constitutive practices revealed in interactional processes. There is a very sharp contrast here not only with most qualitative interview studies but also with most qualitative inquiry of other kinds.[6]

So, despite initial appearances, Potter and Hepburn are not arguing just that researchers using interviews must pay more attention to the interview process, nor simply that it is preferable to base analysis on 'naturalistic materials'. Rather, they are insisting that the only viable or legitimate focus for research is on the interactional practices through which the social world is constituted. Most of the topics typically studied within psychology, and social science more generally, are ruled out by this stance, because these presuppose that there are cognitive and other objects that exist independently of how they are formulated in and through discursive practices, that these causally or intentionally shape human behaviour, and that informants can provide information about them and/or researchers observe them.

---

6 In the case of ethnography, the contrast was neatly demonstrated in Wieder's (1974) book *Language and Social Reality*, in which the author first provides an ethnographic account of how an informal set of rules seems to operate among inmates of a 'halfway house' for ex-prisoners, shaping their behaviour, for example in ruling out their giving information about other inmates to the staff. Then, in the second half of the book, Wieder adopts a more constructionist approach (like Potter and Hepburn influenced by ethnomethodology), in which the focus is on how inmates formulate their actions through appeal to this code, and in the process continually formulate and reformulate the code itself. Here the code cannot serve as an explanatory factor accounting for inmates' behaviour since it is recognised to be part of how the meaning of that behaviour is ongoingly constituted.

Commentaries on Potter and Hepburn's article and their response

As I noted earlier, Potter and Hepburn's article was accompanied by three commentaries. The first came from a researcher who has championed the use of in-depth interviews for phenomenological analysis in psychology (Smith 2008; Smith *et al.* 2009). He expresses sympathy for their general argument, and for some of their recommendations, agreeing about the need to pay more attention to interview processes. However, he comments that the authors privilege one type of qualitative work (that characteristic of conversation analysis and discursive psychology), and that key aspects of their argument do not apply to other kinds. For example, he rejects the requirements Potter and Hepburn lay down about transcription, and their suggestion that, generally speaking, it is better to rely upon naturalistic data. Indeed, he insists that 'interviews are particularly useful for in-depth idiographic studies exploring how participants are making sense of experiences happening to them' (Smith 2005: 311). He concludes that while such research requires careful attention to the interview process, this is no barrier to drawing conclusions about people's perspectives and lives.

The second commentator also accepts some of Potter and Hepburn's arguments but insists, once again, that they privilege a particular approach. However, where Smith more or less accepts the value of that approach, Hollway (2005) suggests that it is preoccupied with 'the most inconsequential and least important' (Hollway 2005: 313) aspects of social interaction. Drawing on psychoanalysis as part of a psycho-social approach, she argues that the kind of work done by Potter and Hepburn neglects the role of what she calls 'subconscious positioning' (Hollway 2005: 312). As part of this, she claims that 'the meaning of any part of an interview (or conversation) inheres in the whole, so that extracts of text can never function satisfactorily as whole units for analysis, only as selected bits of evidence (and counterevidence, where appropriate) for an argument that is being constructed bearing in mind this larger whole' (Hollway 2005: 312). She also criticizes Potter and Hepburn for assuming that there is some single form of transcription, namely that used by conversation analysts, which fully captures the nature of particular stretches of social interaction. She argues that different sorts of transcript are required for different theoretical purposes, to bring out different aspects of social process. In particular, what she is objecting to is the way in which, through the kind of transcription that Potter and Hepburn recommend, the focus of inquiry is narrowed to what is 'observable'.

By contrast with the other two commentators, Mishler (2005) dismisses most of Potter and Hepburn's argument as a form of 'naïve realism', 'positivism' or 'behaviourism', claiming that in this respect it is characteristic of recent developments in conversation analysis, which has become transformed into a technical enterprise.[7] Like Hollway, he challenges the assumption that there is 'some atheoretical way of transcribing that will provide a "full", i.e. complete and accurate transcription [...]' (Mishler 2005: 317). Indeed, he argues that it may sometimes be necessary to reduce the amount of detail in a transcript to bring into relief the features that are relevant to a particular study.[8] On the basis of this, he questions the requirements they lay down regarding transcription. And, like the other two commentators, he insists on the value of interviews as a source of data for qualitative research, arguing that the problems these involve must be addressed and dealt with in practical terms, not on the basis of abstract methodological argument.

Interestingly, Mishler's use of interviews in his own research, employing what he calls narrative analysis, is close in some important respects to what Potter and Hepburn recommend (Mishler 1991 and 2004). He too has complained, for example, about how in much qualitative analysis using interviews 'the sequence and patterning of successive exchanges is deleted from the analysis' (Mishler 2004: 23). And his work involves 'the use of a systematic transcription procedure that represents paralinguistic features of speech and the interaction between speakers'. Furthermore, he includes transcripts in the text so as to provide readers 'with the evidence on which I base my interpretations' (Mishler 2004: 20). However, there is at least one key respect in which he differs from Potter and Hepburn: he believes that through attention to the narrative structure of interview data it is possible to learn about the lives of the people interviewed and how these have been shaped by social circumstances. In other words, he does not see a constructionist emphasis on the constitutive role of discourse as blocking the social scientific use of interview data to understand people's

7 This is a common criticism. For a sophisticated example from within ethnomethodology, cited by Mishler, see Lynch (1993: ch.6).

8 In their article Potter and Hepburn acknowledge the 'power' of this idea but counter that they find the reverse argument 'more compelling' (Potter and Hepburn 2005: 288).

lives. Quite the reverse, he believes that the metaphors and other tropes that they use in interviews can tell us a great deal about what has shaped their lives and how they responded and adapted to this.

In replying to these commentaries, Potter and Hepburn (2005) insist that their critics have not provided an effective response to their arguments. They state that they recognize that different kinds of transcription are appropriate for different purposes. And they dismiss accusations of positivism, and seek to show that their arguments have stronger and more significant implications than the commentators have recognized. They say, for example, that they are not against researchers having different goals from those characteristic of their own work, but insist that satisfying any goal 'is likely to require an understanding of *precisely what the interviewee is saying*' (Potter and Hepburn 2005: 321) and that the sort of transcription they recommend is the best means for achieving this, since it allows attention to be given to the interactional accomplishment of interview talk. In effect, then, they continue to maintain that the kind of detailed attention to 'observable' processes that they themselves practice is (at the very least) an essential prerequisite for any rigorous form of analysis using interview data.

Reflections on the dispute

At face value, what we have in this debate are differences in view about what is required if sound inferences are to be made on the basis of interview data. One source of these is a difference between Potter and Hepburn, on the one hand, and their critics, on the other, in what might be called 'methodological severity' (Hammersley and Gomm 2008): in other words, in judgments about how serious a threat the interactive and co-constructed character of interviews poses to the validity of inferences drawn about perspectives and practices outside the interview context. As we noted, Potter and Hepburn suggest that there is a real danger that the researcher-as-interviewer prompts responses from informants that are largely structured by the analytic framework he or she has adopted. In effect, they are claiming that while qualitative researchers adopt unstructured interviewing to minimize reactivity, in fact the responses they get from informants may be just as strongly shaped by the interviewer and the interview context as those of respondents in structured interviews. Most qualitative researchers would disagree, insisting that there is, at the very least, an important difference in degree here.

At the same time, as we have seen, such 'methodological severity', or empiricism, is not the only or the most significant difference between Potter and Hepburn and their critics. There is also a fundamental discrepancy in assumptions about the nature of the social world and how we can understand it. For Potter and Hepburn, drawing on ethnomethodological conversation analysis, there are neither psychological nor social objects existing in the world that shape human behaviour, or that 'lie behind' the accounts that people provide. All objects are constituted in and through specific interactional processes taking place on particular occasions, whether in interviews or in other settings; they have no existence apart from this.

At root, then, what we have in this particular debate is a clash between very different assumptions about the nature of the social world, what kind of knowledge it is possible for psychological (and social) research to produce, and about the means that would be required to achieve this. However, with the partial exception of Mishler, the fundamental character of the conflict tends to be obscured by both sides.[9]

The critique of urban ethnography

The second dispute we will look at is very different in focus from the first, and in the issues it raises. It was prompted by a lengthy, and highly critical, review (Wacquant 2002) of three ethnographic studies of impoverished African-Americans living in inner-city contexts in the United States, those of Duneier (1999), Anderson (1999) and Newman (1999). The three authors then responded to this critique (Duneier 2002, Anderson 2002 and Newman 2002).[10]

Background to the dispute

To start with, we should note that there is a back-story to this debate. Anderson (2002: 1577) reports that 'long before its publication in the *American Journal of Sociology* in 2002', Wacquant had 'been busy

9 For one attempt to sketch a mid-position between radical critics of interviewing like Potter and Hepburn and the widespread complacency about its capacities that they rightly criticise, see Hammersley and Gomm (2008).

10 See also the debate over Wacquant's own book *Body and Soul* (2004), in the pages of the journal *Symbolic Interaction*: Adler and Adler (2005), May (2005), Sanders (2005), Wacquant (2005).

distributing his attack around the globe and across the profession'. Even more importantly, this dispute should be seen against the background of previous work (and disputes) in the field concerned. There is a long history of qualitative, especially ethnographic, studies of working class and poor urban communities. For instance, one of the aims of Chicago sociologists in the 1920s and 1930s was to map the character of various parts of their city, inhabited by people in very different material circumstances and with very different backgrounds, characteristics, preoccupations, and attitudes (Bulmer 1984). As part of this, the Chicagoans investigated 'slum' and 'skid row' areas, and since that time there have been many other studies focusing on inner-city, poor, urban communities in other parts of the United States, and elsewhere.

One long-running theme in this body of research has, of course, been about the factors that generate and sustain poverty. Wilson (2009) formulates this in terms of differential emphasis upon structural or cultural factors: in other words, on social factors that affect the situations faced by people (such as restriction to low paid jobs, unemployment, poor quality housing, etc) or on factors to do with differences in how people respond to situations (notably, their local cultures, attitudes, beliefs, knowledge and skills). And discussions about the role of these two types of factor have been preoccupied not just with their relative causal power but also with what are taken to be their political and moral implications. A stress on social structural factors (such as de-industrialisation, punitive government policies, etc) tends to undercut any blaming of poor communities for their circumstances but at the same time may seem to portray them as passive victims. By contrast, emphasizing cultural factors is often viewed as recognizing that people can respond in creative ways to their situations, that they are *not* passive, but also as opening up the possibility of 'blaming the victim'. Such debates have a long history (see Matza 1967).[11]

Much of the debate immediately prior to Wacquant's critique had focused on the concept of an underclass. Wacquant and Wilson (1993) put forward an argument that pointed to the importance of structural factors producing inner-city, black communities that are largely separated

---

11 There is no automatic connection between emphasis on one or other of these factors and particular political and social implications: people can, for instance, be portrayed as passive victims of the culture into which they have been socialised. Gomm (2001) has documented the discursive ploys generated by oscillation between these two emphases.

from mainstream society in material terms. However, the notion of an underclass had also been taken up by some social scientists and political commentators who formulated it in cultural terms, sometimes in ways that denied or downplayed the role of structural factors; thereby, it was claimed, blaming these communities for their own impoverishment. Here is Wilson's (1993a: 2) summary of these developments in the United States:

> During the decade of the 1970s, significant changes occurred in ghetto neighbourhoods of large central cities; however they were not carefully monitored or researched by social scientists during the 1970s and early 1980s. [This was because in] the aftermath of the controversy over Daniel Patrick Moynihan's report on the black family [in the late 1960s] scholars, particularly liberal scholars, tended to shy away from researching any behavior that could be construed as stigmatizing or unflattering to inner-city minority residents. [...] Accordingly, [...] the problems of social dislocation in the inner-city ghetto did not attract serious research attention. This left [the field] open to conservative analysts who, without benefit of actual field research in the inner city, put their own peculiar stamp on the problem, so much so that the dominant image of the underclass became one of people with serious character flaws entrenched by a welfare subculture and who have only themselves to blame for their social position in society.

Wacquant's critique

Wacquant (2002: 1469) summarises the three books he is criticising as follows:

> Mitchell Duneier's *Sidewalk* tracks the trials and tribulations of black homeless book vendors and magazine scavengers who ply their trade in a touristy section of Lower Manhattan; Elijah Anderson's *Code of the Street* chronicles the raging battle between 'street' and 'decent' families in the ghetto of Philadelphia; and Katherine Newman's *No Shame in My Game* depicts the gallant struggles of the 'working poor' of Harlem to uphold the hallowed values of thrift, family, and community in the bowels of the deregulated service economy.

From this Wacquant (2002: 1469) moves very quickly into evaluation:

> These books assemble a mass of rich and nuanced empirical data variously drawn from firsthand observation, in-depth interviews, life stories, and institutional reports gathered over years of fieldwork conducted individually or in a team. They would have greatly advanced our knowledge and understanding of the ground-level social dynamics and lived experience of urban marginality and racial division in the United States at century's end, were it not for their eager embrace of the clichés of public debate (albeit in inverted form), the pronounced discordance between interpretation and the evidence they offer, and the thick coat of moralism in which their analyses are wrapped, which together severely limit the questions they raise and the answers they give.

Wacquant (2002: 1469–70) fills out these criticisms as follows:

> Thus *Sidewalk* proffers a sprawling stockpile of data without any theory to organize it and strives, by default, to bring these data to bear on a crime-and-policing issue that they are ill-suited to address; *Code of the Street* is animated by a thesis, that proximate mentoring makes a difference in the fate of ghetto residents, that is glaringly disconnected from, even invalidated by, its own findings; and *No Shame in My Game* subordinates both observations and theorization to public policy considerations, such as the ideological dispute over 'family values', that are so constricting that it ends up slighting its own discoveries and reading like a business tract in praise of low-wage work.
>
> More significantly, all three authors put forth truncated and distorted accounts of their object due to their abiding wish to articulate and even celebrate the fundamental goodness – honesty, decency, frugality – of America's urban poor. To do this Duneier *sanitizes* the actions and neighborhood impact of sidewalk bookselling by systematically downplaying or suppressing information that would taint the saintly image of the vendors he wishes to project; Anderson *dichotomizes* ghetto residents into good and bad, 'decent' and 'street', and makes himself the spokesman and advocate of the former; and Newman *glamorizes* the skills and deeds of her low-wage workers, extolling their submission to servile labor as evidence of their inner devotion to the country's ordained 'work ethic'. All three authors make the urban poor, and to be more

> exact the *black* subproletariat of the city, into *paragons of morality* because they remain locked within the *prefabricated problematic* of public stereotypes and policy punditry, for which it is the only guise under which this subproletariat is deemed 'presentable'.

Identifying the grounds of disagreement

At face value, Wacquant is challenging these studies in terms of the quality of their academic scholarship, in other words according to principles that would be shared by most social scientists. He complains that they did not deploy an adequate theory to organize their data; that their conclusions are not supported by the evidence they provide, and may even be contradicted by it; and that these faults derive, in large part, from bias caused by the fact that the authors set out to challenge prevailing ideas about an underclass – seeking to undercut public assumptions about the immorality of poor, black inhabitants of inner-city areas and to reveal their commitment to 'respectable' ways of life. Most qualitative researchers, and social scientists more generally, would surely want studies to display adequate theorization, conclusions well-supported by evidence, and the avoidance of bias.

The rejoinders by Duneier, Anderson, and Newman also operate within these terms: they are largely concerned with showing that Wacquant has misrepresented their work.[12] Thus, Duneier argues that Wacquant uses selective quotation to produce a misleading impression of what he was claiming in *Sidewalk*. For example, at one point Wacquant refers to 'Duneier's uncritical acceptance of his informants' self-portraits', and provides the following quotation from Duneier in support: 'I have *never* doubted *any* of the things Hakim told me about his life.' (Wacquant 2002: 1478). However, the footnote to Duneier's book that this comes from reads as follows: 'Although I have never doubted any of the things Hakim told me about his life, in conducting this study I have looked upon it as my responsibility to check salient things people tell me about themselves before reporting them.' (Duneier 1999: 360). Thus, Wacquant has added misleading emphasis and excised material that counts against his interpretation. And, Duneier goes on to explain how he asked Hakim to apply for a copy of his college records and to obtain official employment

12 For reasons of space, I will focus primarily on Wacquant's critique of Duneier and the latter's response to this.

information about the last firm for which he worked, so as to validate what he had claimed; reporting that 'everything checked out' (Duneier 1999: 360; Duneier 2002: 1553). In this and other cases, it appears that Wacquant's critique involves serious misrepresentation.

However, this is not the most significant aspect of this dispute for my purposes here. I suggest that while it may seem as if the protagonists are all engaged in the same enterprise, and are therefore simply disagreeing about how well it has been pursued in particular studies, this is not in fact the case. For example, if we take Wacquant's first criticism, what he means by 'theory', and how he views its role in 'organising the data', are almost certainly at odds with the assumptions about theory and evidence on which Duneier, and perhaps also Anderson and Newman, operate.

'Theory' is a notoriously problematic term. While most, though not all, social scientists are concerned with producing and drawing on theory, and emphasize its importance, in practice they often use the word to refer to different things: from broad methodological philosophies, through comprehensive social theories, to specific explanatory ideas (Hammersley 2012b). Wacquant seems to assume that any ethnographic study should be located within a macro-level theory that identifies the dominant social forces and structural patterns that characterize the wider society. And he also seems to believe that such a theory must precede and structure any empirical research: that the phenomena to be investigated must be theoretically constituted (Wacquant 2005; Bourdieu and Wacquant 1992). A sign of this is his reference to grounded theorizing as an 'epistemological fairy tale' (Wacquant 2005: 1481), the implication being that it is a form of empiricism.

Indeed, Wacquant had already put forward a theoretical framework for the study of inner-city black communities (see, for example, Wacquant 1997 and 2008). It is largely on the basis of this that he accuses Duneier, and his fellow ethnographers, of neglecting wider structural forces in favour of focusing on local cultural factors. He charges them with 'blindness to issues of class power' and a 'stubborn disregard for the deep and multisided involvements [...] of the state in producing the dereliction and human wretchedness they sensibly portray [...]' (Wacquant 2002: 1470). Specifically in the case of Duneier, Wacquant claims that he 'does not discuss the structural forces – the desocialization of labor, the erosion of the patriarchal household, the retrenchment of the welfare state, the criminalization of the urban poor, the conflation of blackness and dangerousness in public space – that directly shape and bound the material and symbolic space within which the vendors [studied by Duneier] operate' (Wacquant 2002: 1480).

As we saw in Chapter 2, this emphasis on the structuring role of macro theory is a central feature of a 'critical' orientation, and this is more or less the stance that Wacquant adopts. Another closely related feature is the assumption that the commonsense ideas prevalent within a society are likely to be ideological – in other words, both false and serving regressive social interests. For this reason, these ideas should not be used as a framework for social analysis, they themselves must be challenged and explained. And it is a key part of the task of theory to do this. Thus, Wacquant criticizes Duneier and the others for their 'naïve acceptance of ordinary categories of perception as categories of analysis' (Wacquant 2002: 1470). He asks: 'Why does Duneier swallow whole the sing-song claim of his subjects that they "made a conscious decision to 'respect' society by scavenging trash or panhandling (instead of breaking into parked cars or selling drugs)" [...]?' (Wacquant 2002: 1481).[13] As this makes clear, Wacquant, like Potter and Hepburn, does not believe that people are 'experts on their lives', although for very different reasons from them.

By contrast, Duneier seems committed to a rather different methodological approach, where the starting point is a particular research topic and the selection of a specific location or group of people that allows its investigation. Here, theoretical ideas play the role of tools that can be deployed and developed *in so far as they make sense of what is going on and enable us to answer the evolving research questions* (Duneier 2002: 1566–7). Furthermore, for him, the perspectives and experience of participants are an essential starting point for understanding what is happening in a setting.

There seem to be several points of difference with Wacquant here. First, the theoretical resources that Duneier employs are multiple rather than forming a single, closely-structured framework. Secondly, Duneier regards selection from and development of the theoretical resources available to the researcher as an inductive process, with what is discovered in the

13 Wacquant's work has been strongly influenced by the work of Bourdieu (see Bourdieu and Wacquant 1992). However, Cole and Dumas (2010) argue that the relationship between analytic and commonsense perspectives is treated as more complex in the book that Bourdieu and Wacquant produced together, and in Bourdieu's work generally, than it is in Wacquant's critique of Duneier, Anderson and Newman.

field playing a guiding role. Thirdly, the concepts and understandings of the people studied are treated as potentially providing key information and insights, even though they are not to be adopted uncritically. Thus, for Duneier, any wider picture of how societal forces are affecting the setting investigated must be generated out of detailed study of it and of the perspectives of participants. In short, a prior comprehensive theory is not required, indeed it is not desirable since it could operate as a set of blinkers. Instead, the relevance and validity of any explanatory ideas must emerge from detailed empirical investigation of the particular case.

Thus it is not that Duneier ignores structural conditions in *Sidewalk*, but he does place primary emphasis on local factors, seeing these as playing a significant role in mediating wider social forces, so that the relevance and effects of the latter can be discovered only through local investigation. Moreover, he believes that much is to be learned by the ethnographer from the experience and perspectives of the people being studied. What is at issue here, then, is not differential emphasis on cultural or structural factors, but rather differences in assumptions about the nature and role of theory, about the relative emphasis that should be given to macro and micro factors, about how these are related to one another, and about the proper relationship between analytic and commonsense understandings.

As this should make clear, Duneier's approach shows strong signs of the influence of interpretivism, and *Sidewalk* was, indeed, largely focused on documenting and explaining the experience of a specific group of people. Indeed, he places particular emphasis upon what he calls 'showing the people'. He has criticized much previous qualitative research for neglecting this:

> If you are going to get at the humanity of people, you can't just have a bunch of disembodied thoughts that come out of subjects' mouths in interviews without ever developing characters [...]. (Duneier and Back 2006: 554).

In line with this idiographic orientation, Duneier includes photographs in his book, and uses people's real names, where they have agreed to this. He writes:

> Being able to show the people in photographs, rather than keeping them anonymous, lends a certain kind of immediacy to the people as people and makes it possible to really conceive of them as full human beings [...]. (Duneier and Back 2006: 554)

Interestingly, one of the ways in which Wacquant (2002: 1525) formulates his criticisms of Duneier is to accuse the latter of recognizing no 'epistemological divide' between sociological research and journalism. In response, Duneier acknowledges that there are some similarities, singling out a concern with checking evidence, but he insists that there are important differences:

> My ethnography [...] has other commitments that most journalists do not share: being public about procedures and clear about uncertainties, presenting alternative interpretations and counterevidence, considering rival hypotheses, striving to achieve replicability, seeking to be aware of investigator effects, and using fieldwork to modify and improve theory.

As we have seen, Wacquant also criticises Duneier and the others for 'moralism'. What this amounts to, in large part, is the claim that the account of the lives of street vendors that Duneier provides is biased: that it de-emphasises or reinterprets those aspects of their lives that would generally be regarded as morally unacceptable, and that it gives undue attention to those that are taken to show the vendors in a good light. This is a charge that Duneier vigorously denies.

What is of interest here is that this criticism could be taken to imply that Wacquant is committed to documenting the workings of society from a non-moral or value-neutral perspective. Yet this is far from the case. What he is objecting to is what he sees as the failure of Duneier and the other ethnographers to locate their work within the moral framework provided by the sort of comprehensive theory that he believes is necessary. Thus, Wacquant certainly does not resist engaging in evaluation himself: he criticizes state policies and the structural inequalities built into US society, for example the way in which the inhabitants of black inner-city communities are restricted to 'lousy' jobs (Wacquant 2002: 1472) or deprived of any legitimate income at all. And, elsewhere, he has himself provided a highly value-laden view of the lives of African-Americans in black ghettoes and of the social forces 'incarcerating' them there (Wacquant 2009).

This might seem to imply that what is at stake is a clash of substantive value perspectives about US society. Yet it is not clear that the two authors differ very greatly in terms of their substantive values. The real difference between them can be clarified by reference to a very influential article by a researcher whose position is quite similar to that of Duneier. As we saw in Chapter 1, Becker's (1967) 'Whose side are we on?' is frequently cited as suggesting that social research should be partisan: that it must support some particular social group or political position against others, more or less in the manner of 'critical' research. However, a careful reading of Becker's article makes clear that this is not his view (see Hammersley 2000: ch.3). He argues that the researcher's primary commitment should be to document what is actually happening in the social world, rather than setting out to criticize it. He argues that this requires strenuous effort to avoid taking over the perspectives that are dominant within a society, *and* to take seriously the experience and perspectives of those who are at the bottom of the 'hierarchy of credibility' within that society. At the same time, he insists on the importance of avoiding what he calls 'sentimentality', one aspect of which would be a refusal to investigate issues that the researcher finds politically or ethically uncomfortable, for example whether the behaviour of marginalized groups matches mainstream stereotypes of them. Becker writes:

> Whatever side we are on, we must use our techniques impartially enough that a belief to which we are especially sympathetic could be proved untrue. We must always inspect our work carefully enough to know whether our techniques and theories are open enough to allow that possibility (Becker 1967: 246).

While Becker assumes that research following this pattern will have politically progressive social consequences, he does *not* believe that researchers should set out to support any particular side, or indeed that they should act directly to promote such consequences. This seems to be Duneier's position too. Certainly, he is primarily concerned with documenting rather than evaluating the behaviour of the people he studied. And he is keen to avoid conventional assumptions biasing his account. While he clearly hoped that his research would dispel stereotypes and thereby lead to better policies, it was not directly geared to bringing about these changes, but rather to providing a true account of the vendors' lives and of the factors that shape them.[14]

In other words, Duneier seeks to maintain some detachment for his research from political struggles over racial discrimination and poverty. By

---

14 His 'moralism', to the extent that this label applies, amounts to an interest in how people relate to moral values, and a concern to establish a relationship with the people he was studying that was significantly more egalitarian than in some previous ethnographies, see Duneier and Back (2005).

contrast, 'critical' researchers deny that there is any scope for such 'detachment', they insist that, whether researchers are aware of it or not, their work always amounts to some kind of political intervention. Furthermore, Wacquant seems to assume not only that high quality research will have desirable political effects but also that any piece of research having what he takes to be undesirable political implications must be false. Thus, for him there is an intrinsic connection between what he sees as methodological defects in Duneier's work and the political implications he believes it carries (see Loader and Sparks 2010: 406–9). His fundamental complaint is that it serves to reinforce the prevailing ideological framework in terms of which urban poverty is publicly discussed. He writes: 'One could hardly formulate a better brief for continuing the state policies of urban abandonment, social disinvestment, workfare, and "prisonfare" that have spawned the mounting social refuse strewn on the streets of the U.S. metropolis.' (Wacquant 2002: 1485–6). He argues that these ethnographic accounts distract attention from the fundamental causes of poverty, in effect suggesting that if poor people would only take proper responsibility for their lives they could work their way out of poverty.

So, the key difference here concerns the role that Wacquant sees social research as playing and that he believes it should play. This is not just a matter of what role researchers might adopt, in terms of how they define the task of inquiry, but also of the role that is, if you like, thrust upon them: what is involved is not simply the intentions of the ethnographers whose work he is discussing, but rather what objective function their work serves in the wider society. Any idea of detachment seems to be rejected by Wacquant, as both impossible in practice and unethical as an ideal.

This is illustrated at one point where he refers to a previous debate from the 1960s, in which the work of Becker and some other Chicago-School sociologists of the time was criticized. He writes that:

> just as the romantic ethnographies of the cool, the marginal, and the lowly produced during the progressive sixties in the style of the second Chicago School were organically tied to the liberal politics of America's semi-welfare state and its then-expanding "social-problems complex" (Gouldner 1973), the neo-romantic tales spun by Duneier, Anderson, and Newman at the close of the regressive nineties suggest that U.S. sociology is now tied and party to the ongoing construction of the neoliberal state and its

> "carceral-assistential complex" for the punitive management of the poor, on and off the street (Wacquant 1999: 83–94) (1470–1).

Here Wacquant is aligning his critique of the work of Duneier, Anderson, and Newman with Gouldner's criticisms of the work of Becker and others in an earlier period. For Gouldner, as for Wacquant, social research must be understood as playing a reflexive role within the wider society: unless it is specifically directed at resisting wider social forces it will inadvertently serve those forces, irrespective of whether this was intended by the researchers concerned.

So, it seems that Wacquant believes that the primary responsibility of the researcher is to orient her or his work in relation to the current political situation in such a way that it will have desirable political implications and consequences. His main objection to the research he criticizes is that it does not do this, and therefore reinforces the socio-political status quo. However, he believes that this is intimately related to the methodological defects that he sees in this research, in the sense that only if research has this orientation, operating within an appropriate theoretical framework, will it be methodologically sound.

What this shows is that the methodological criticisms that Wacquant makes of these studies, which are the main focus of the three authors' responses to him, are secondary to more basic disagreements between them. Like Potter and Hepburn in the first dispute I discussed, Wacquant is laying down a more severe set of criteria regarding what should be treated as reliable evidence and inference, and one that relies upon distinctive assumptions about the proper nature of inquiry; though, of course, his assumptions are very different from theirs. His critique is based upon a notion of 'critical' sociology as a discipline that is both scientific and politically engaged, these two aspects being closely interrelated (see Bourdieu and Wacquant 1992: 47).[15]

---

15 However, it seems to me that his assumptions about the nature of this relationship are rather unclear. As we saw in Chapter 2, for Marx the connection between science and politics lay in its capacity to identify the potential for realising genuine human nature and the barriers to achieving this. It is not clear whether Bourdieu and Waquant accept this or rely upon some alternative means of deriving 'ought' from 'is'. In my view none of the proposed strategies for doing this are successful. For discussion of the sophisticated attempt to solve this problem proposed by critical realists, see Hammersley (2009).

We can see here, then, that this dispute, like the previous one, is underpinned by some quite fundamental philosophical differences: concerning the purpose and character of social research, the nature of social scientific knowledge and how it can best be produced, the role of political values in the research enterprise, and (following on from this) the social role and political responsibilities of the researcher.[16]

Conclusion

In this chapter we have looked at two important disputes among qualitative researchers that are very different in focus and in the issues they raise, as well as in the sorts of approach championed by the protagonists. Yet, what both these disputes show, I suggest, is that qualitative research is currently riven by a range of fundamental differences in methodological philosophy and practical orientation, albeit ones that are often partly obscured through appeals to common issues. Thus, Potter and Hepburn seek to persuade researchers of all kinds that there are serious problems with using interviews, appealing to what they present as common ground. However, they base their arguments on assumptions about the nature of psychological and social phenomena, and how we can understand them, that are informed by radical constructionism, and at the same time by an empiricism which demands that any analysis is tied down to the observable details of interaction. These assumptions are sharply at odds with those adopted by many other qualitative researchers, including the commentators on their article.

Similarly, Wacquant appeals to various kinds of inaccuracy and methodological weakness in the studies he reviews. Yet his critique is motivated in large part by a 'critical' orientation that, it seems to me, the people whose work he is reviewing do not share. He insists on the importance of a general theory about the nature of US society that provides him with a framework within which both to describe and explain the behaviour of African-Americans who live in inner-city communities, *and* to evaluate the various structural forces and agents involved. And he insists that sociological work must be directed at challenging existing society so as to bring

16 By contrast with the approach I have taken here, Cole and Dumas (2010), while recognising important differences between Wacquant and Duneier, emphasise what they see as similarities.

about change, and above all it must not reinforce the dominant ideology. However, those whose work he is criticizing do not fully share this view of the character and role of social research, even if they have similar values.

Conclusion

In the opening chapter of this book I highlighted some of the complexities involved in answering the question 'What is qualitative research?'. My aim was to show the uncertain and contested nature of any answer to that question. This is true even of attempts to provide a conventional definition – concerned with how the term is currently used, or with the sorts of work generally included under this heading. It is even more true of ideas about how 'qualitative inquiry' *ought to be* defined.

We saw that while it is possible to identify a number of features that studies which are typically classified as qualitative usually share, as contrasted with quantitative work, it is impossible to identify a set of *essential* characteristics. It is also important to note that many of these shared features are matters of degree: such as the *extent* to which the data are structured at the point of collection, and the *number* of cases investigated. This should warn us that trying to draw a very sharp line, *at the level of practice*, between qualitative and quantitative work is problematic, even though the degree of variation is considerable.

At the same time there are major differences in terms of methodological philosophy. To one degree or another, qualitative research is shaped by very different ideas – about the nature of social phenomena and how they can be understood – from quantitative work. But later chapters also revealed that conflicting methodological philosophies have generated divergent modes of inquiry, and major disputes, *within* qualitative research. Indeed, these divisions are today probably deeper and more intractable than any between qualitative and quantitative work.

In part, the diversity in orientation has arisen simply from expansion of the social sciences over the second half of the twentieth century and into the twenty-first. During this period there has been: a huge increase in the number of social scientists, and in the amount of research, across the world; a proliferation of substantive fields of investigation, along with the development of distinctive theoretical and methodological ideas within them; the emergence of new disciplines, such as cultural studies and childhood studies, and a migration of some parts of existing ones – including from history, geography, and psychology – into a broader interdisciplinary field of sociocultural research; the re-emergence of social theory as relatively autonomous from empirical research, but at the same time very influential upon it; the impact of social movements of various kinds, from feminism to disability activism; and increased pressures for public and practical engagement of social scientific work deriving from governments and commercial sources. The effect of these factors has been to produce a massively expanded, highly complex, and only very loosely structured terrain, in which different parts of social science have developed and devolved in many different directions. To some degree, the heterogeneous forms that qualitative work now takes reflects this process of diversification in the social sciences more generally, and perhaps also the weakness of its boundaries with forms of social and political practice.

As is often the case when there is rapid differentiation, there have also been some moves towards reintegration, though these are necessarily partial in character. For example, some influential commentators have sought to define 'qualitative research' as a 'field of inquiry in its own right' (Denzin and Lincoln 2011: 3). It is presented as a trans-disciplinary movement that draws on a mélange of interpretivist, 'critical', and constructionist ideas, in which 'new forms' of research presentation are to be employed in the promotion of 'social justice'. Thus Denzin and Lincoln report that:

> the qualitative research community consists of groups of globally dispersed persons who are attempting to implement a critical interpretive approach that will help them (and others) make sense of the terrifying conditions that define daily life at the first decade of this new century. These individuals employ constructivist, critical theory, feminist, queer, and critical race theory, as well as cultural studies models of interpretation. (Denzin and Lincoln 2011: xii)

Whether its aim is formulated as promoting 'arts-based research' or a 'sacred science' (Denzin and Lincoln 1994: 582–3) this movement brings together many qualitative researchers from different fields. At the same time, it also excludes or marginalizes a great deal of what I have included in this book under the heading of 'qualitative research'.

A very different integrative approach is the 'mixed methods' movement, which stresses the complementarity of qualitative and quantitative methods and the benefits of combining them within particular research projects. Yet, it should be clear from earlier chapters that the discrepant forms that qualitative research now takes, and the rationales associated with these, cannot be easily reconciled with one another, nor with the predominant orientation of quantitative researchers. 'Mixing' quantitative and qualitative methods frequently involves abandoning key assumptions associated with many sorts of qualitative work. There is nothing wrong with this, in principle, but there is little agreement within the mixed methods movement about what methodological philosophy ought to underpin it (Tashakkori and Teddlie 2010). Furthermore, in practice, there is a tendency in mixed methods work to assimilate the use of qualitative methods into the framework of assumptions characteristic of quantitative work – yet these require just as much careful scrutiny (see Hammersley 2012a).

All this raises some very difficult questions:

- Is the label 'qualitative research' helpful any longer? Does it pick out a reasonably coherent set of practices and/or methodological ideas that are sound? In short, does it make a distinction that is of value?
- What attitude should be taken towards the heterogeneity of qualitative research today? Should we be tolerant of approaches that are discrepant with our own, or should the boundaries of what is legitimate be policed, and if so how?
- What should be the operational goal of qualitative researchers, and for what should they be held accountable? Should the aim be to bring about socio-political change, as proposed by 'critical' approaches, or to subvert claims to expert knowledge and recover subjugated voices, as some constructionists suggest? Or is the task solely to produce knowledge? If knowledge is the goal, should this be idiographic or more general in character? Should the aim of research be to capture embodied 'lived experience' or to produce objective answers to research questions?
- In the face of constructionist arguments, can any claim to produce scientific knowledge about the social world be warranted? If so, what forms of such knowledge are viable? And how do they differ from journalism, literature, or art?
- Is social science *desirable*, as a specialized source of knowledge about the world? Or is it inevitably an oppressive disciplinary technology?

Qualitative researchers today would, of course, give conflicting answers to these questions. I can only sketch my own response in what remains of this Conclusion.

For me, qualitative research is nothing if it is not social science. And this implies that it is distinctive as a form of activity precisely in being directed exclusively at the operational goal of producing propositional knowledge (answers to specific, factual questions), albeit knowledge that has some value, either in terms of being relevant to important issues to do with policy or practice in some field or in relation to general human concerns (Hammersley 2011).

Adopting this position means dismissing some elements of all the methodological philosophies introduced in Chapter 2, while retaining others. One element that must be excluded is the idea, central to a 'critical' approach, that research should be designed to challenge the *status quo* or to bring about social change. These tasks are no more a proper part of the responsibility of researchers than is seeking to preserve the status quo or to serve national or religious interests.

Equally problematic, in my view, is the notion, at the heart of some kinds of interpretivism, that the goal of social research is to understand unique individuals and to present accounts of their lives and experience. This is the task of biography and fictional writing, and there is an important difference between this and the proper use that social scientists can make of biographical materials, life histories, or fictional depictions. The sole aim of social science must be to produce knowledge about social institutions, policies, and/or processes, their character, sources, or consequences.

Similarly, those elements of constructionism that question the very possibility of knowledge – in general, or about the social world in particular – must be rejected, simply on the grounds that they are incompatible with a commitment to research. After all, we cannot engage in that activity without assuming the possibility and desirability of knowledge. It may be legitimate to challenge these assumptions, but this cannot be done *as part of* social science. And attempts to do this via appeal to the model of the humanities and arts are misguided, since that complex field is itself divided between those areas of work that are committed to the production of knowledge – such as most historical work and much philosophy – and those that have very different and internally diverse orientations – such as creating artistic or literary works. My point is not that there is anything wrong with these other activities, far from it, only that they have a different character and purpose from research; and we should be clear about which activity we are engaged in, since if we are not we will very likely do neither of them well.

Finally, given that, in practical terms, the difference between qualitative and quantitative methods is a matter of degree, I do not believe that 'qualitative research' is a genuine or useful category – any more than is 'quantitative research'. While, at present, we cannot avoid reliance upon this distinction, we need to move towards a more adequate typology, exploring the various options open to social researchers as regards how they formulate research questions, engage in research design, collect and produce data, analyze it, and report their findings. The qualitative-quantitative divide reifies what is variable, and obscures the scope for combining strategies that can be employed to deal with these different aspects of the research process. In short, we need to find a way of overcoming the quantitative-qualitative divide, of replacing it with a more subtle and realistic set of distinctions that capture variation in research practice better.

Of course, the position I have just sketched is not one that would be accepted by many qualitative researchers today. The issues remain unresolved; so you, dear reader, will have to come to your own conclusions about them.

References

Adler, P. A. and P. Adler (2005) 'Lost in Translation?', *Symbolic Interaction*, 28, 33–435.

Alasuutari, P. (1995) *Researching Culture: Qualitative method and cultural studies*, London, Sage.

Albert, H. (1985) *Treatise on Critical Reason*, Princeton NJ, Princeton University Press.

Anderson E. (Elizabeth) (2011) 'Feminist epistemology and the philosophy of science', Stanford Encyclopedia of Philosophy, Available at (accessed 11.1.12): http://plato.stanford.edu/entries/feminism-epistemology/

Anderson, E. (Elijah) (1999) *Code of the Street: Decency, violence and the moral life of the inner city*, New York, Norton.

Anderson, E. (Elijah) (2002) 'The ideologically driven critique', *American Journal of Sociology*, 107, 6, 1533–50.

Andrews, M., Sclater, S.D., Squire, C. and Treacher, A. (eds) (2000). *Lines of Narrative.* London: Routledge.

Armstrong, G. (1998) *Football Hooligans: knowing the score*, Oxford, Berg.

Ashmore, M. (1989) *The Reflexive Thesis*, Chicago, University of Chicago Press.

Ashmore, M. and Reed, D. (2000) 'Innocence and Nostalgia in Conversation Analysis: The Dynamic Relations of Tape and Transcript', *Forum: Qualitative Research* 1(3), URL (accessed 17 April 2012): http://www.qualitative-research.net/index.php/fqs/article/view/1020

Ashmore, M., MacMillan, K. and Brown, S.D. (2004) '"It's a Scream": Professional Hearing and Tape Fetishism', *Journal of Pragmatics* 36(2): 349–74.

Atkinson, P. (1983) 'Writing ethnography' in H.J.Helle (ed.) *Kultur und Institution*, Berlin, Duncker und Humblot.

Atkinson, P. (1990) *The Ethnographic Imagination: textual construction of reality*, London, Routledge.

Atkinson, P. (1997) 'Narrative Turn or Blind Alley?' *Qualitative Health Research*, 7, 3, 325–344.

Atkinson, P. and Coffey, A. (2002) 'Revisiting the relationship between participant observation and interviewing', in Gubrium, J. F. and Holstein, J. A. (eds.) *Handbook of Interview Research*, Thousand Oaks CA, Sage.

Atkinson, P. and Delamont, S. (eds.) (2004) *Narrative Methods*, Four volumes, London, Sage.

Atkinson, P. and Silverman, D. (1997) 'Kundera's "Immortality": The Interview Society and the Invention of the Self', *Qualitative Inquiry*, 3, 3, 304–325.

Ball, M. and Smith, G. (1992) *Analysing Visual Data*, Beverly Hills CA, Sage.

Banks, M. (2001) *Visual Methods in Social Research*, London, Sage.

Bauman, Z. (2000) *Liquid Modernity*, Cambridge, Polity.

Becker, H. S. (1953) 'Becoming a marihuana user', *American Journal of Sociology*, 59, 3, 235–42.

Becker, H. S. (1955) 'Marihuana use and social control', *Social Problems*, 3, 1, 35–44.

Becker, H. S. (1967) 'Whose side are we on?', *Social Problems*, 14 (Winter) 239–47

Becker, H. S. (1973) *Outsiders*, New York, Free Press.

Becker, H. S. and Geer, B. (1957) 'Participant observation and interviewing: a comparison', *Human Organization*, 16, 3, 28–32.

Bennett, A. and Elman, C. (2006) 'Qualitative Research: Recent Developments in Case Study Methods', *Annual Review of Political Science*, 9, 459–460.

Berger, P. and Luckmann, T. (1967) *The Social Construction of Reality: A treatise in the sociology of knowledge*, New York, Anchor.

Berlin, I. (1954) *Historical Inevitability*, Oxford, Oxford University Press.

Bignell, J. (1997) *Media Semiotics: An introduction*, Manchester, University of Manchester Press.

Bird, A. (2000) *Thomas Kuhn*, Princeton NJ, Princeton University Press.

Bochner, A. and Ellis, C. (eds.) (2002) *Ethnographically speaking: autoethnography, literature, and aesthetics*, Walnut Creek CA, Altamira.

Bogdan, R. (1974) *Being Different: The autobiography of Jane Fry*, London, Wiley.

Bourdieu, P. and Wacquant, L. (1992) *An Invitation to Reflexive Sociology*, Cambridge, Polity.

Brady, H. and Collier, D. (eds.) (2004) *Rethinking Social Inquiry: Diverse tools, shared standards*, Lanham, MD, Rowman and Littlefield.

Brewer, J. (2004) *Sentimental Murder*, London, Harper-Collins.

Brown, R.H. (1989) *A Poetic for Sociology*, Second edition, Chicago, University of Chicago Press.

Bryant, C. (1985) *Positivism in Social Theory and Research*, London, Macmillan.

Bryant, A. and Charmaz, K. (eds.) (2007) *The Sage Handbook of Grounded Theory*, London, Sage.

Bryant, A. and Charmaz, K. (2011) 'Grounded theory', in Williams and Vogt (eds.).

Bryman, A. (2007) 'Barriers to integrating quantitative and qualitative research', *Journal of Mixed Methods Research*, 1, 1–18.

Bryman, A. (2008a) 'The end of the paradigm wars?', in Alasuutari, P., Bickman, L., and Brannen, J. (eds.) *The Sage Handbook of Social Research Methods*, London, Sage.

Bryman, A. (2008b) *Social Research Methods*, Third edition, Oxford, Oxford University Press.

Buford, B. (1991) *Among the Thugs: the experience, and the seduction, of crowd violence*, London, Secker and Warburg.

Bulmer, M. (1984) *The Chicago School of Sociology: Institutionalization, Diversity, and the Rise of Sociological Research*, Chicago, University of Chicago Press.

Burawoy, M. (1987) 'The limits of Wright's analytical Marxism and an alternative', *Berkeley Journal of Sociology*, 32, 51–72.

Burawoy, M. (2005) 'For public sociology', *American Sociological Review*, 70, 1, 4–28.

Burr, V. (2003), *An Introduction to Social Constructionism*, Second edition, London, Routledge.

Burr, V. (2004), 'Constructivism', in M. Lewis-Beck, A. Bryman and T. F. Liao (eds.) *Encyclopedia of Social Science Research Methods*, Thousand Oaks, Sage.

Button, G. and Sharrock, W. (1993), 'A disagreement over agreement and consensus in constructionist sociology', *Journal for the Theory of Social Behaviour*, 23, 1, 1–25.

Caldas-Coulthard, C., and Coulthard, M. (eds.) (1996) *Texts and Practices: Readings in Critical Discourse Analysis*, London, Routledge.

Calvey, D. (2000) 'Getting on the Door and Staying there: A Covert Participant Observational Study of Bouncers', in Lee-Treweek, G. and Linkogle, S. (eds.) *Danger in the field: risk and ethics in social research.* London, Routledge.
Campbell, D. (1975) 'Degrees of freedom and the case study', *Comparative Political Studies*, 8, 2, 178–193.
Charlton, D. (1959) *Positivist thought in France during the Second Empire, 1852–1870*, Oxford, Oxford University Press.
Charmaz, Kathy (2000) 'Grounded Theory: Objectivist and Constructivist Methods' in Denzin, N. and Lincoln, Y. (eds.), *Handbook of Qualitative Research*, 2nd edition (509–535), Thousand Oaks CA, Sage.
Charmaz, K. (2006) *Constructing Grounded Theory*, London, Sage.
Christie, R. (1976) 'Comment on Conflict Methodology', *Sociological Quarterly*, 1, 7, 513–519.
Clifford, J. and Marcus, G. (eds.) (1986) *Writing Culture: The poetics and politics of ethnography*, Berkeley CA, University of California Press.
Cole, S. and Dumas, M. (2010) 'Shadowboxing with the ghost of Bourdieu', Goldsmiths, University of London. Available at (accessed 28.12.11): http://www.gold.ac.uk/media/Cole-Dumasfinalpaper.pdf
Cooper, B., Glaesser, J., Gomm, R., and Hammersley, M. (2012) *Challenging the Qualitative-Quantitative Divide*, London, Continuum.
Cortazzi, M. (1993) *Narrative Analysis*, London, Falmer Press.
Coulter, J. (1999) 'Discourse and mind', *Human Studies*, 22, 163–181.
Coulter, J. (2004) 'What is "Discursive Psychology"?', *Human Studies*, 27, 3, 335–40.
Cressey, D. (1953) *Other People's Money*, Glencoe ILL., Free Press. Second edition, Belmont CA, Wadsworth, 1971.
Cuff, E. (1993) *Problems of Versions in Everyday Situations*, Second edition, Lanham MD, University Press of America.
Culler, J. (2002) *Barthes: a very short introduction*, Oxford University Press.
De Waal, C. (2005) *On Pragmatism*, Belmont CA. Thomson-Wadsworth.
Dean, J. P. and Whyte, W. F. (1958) 'How do you know if the informant is telling the truth?', *Human Organization*, 17, 2, 34–8.
Denzin, N. and Y. Lincoln (eds.) (1994) *Handbook of Qualitative Research*, First edition, Thousand Oaks, CA, Sage.
Denzin, N. and Y. Lincoln (eds.) (2011) *Handbook of Qualitative Research*, fourth edition, Thousand Oaks, CA, Sage.

Denzin, N., Lincoln, Y. and Smith, L. (eds.) (2008) *Handbook of Critical and Indigenous Methodologies*, Los Angeles, Sage.

Deutscher, I. (1973) *What We Say/What We Do: Sentiments and acts*, Glenview IL, Scott, Foresman and Co.

Dey, I. (1999) *Grounding Grounded Theory*, New York, Academic Press.

Dicks, B., Soyinka, B., and Coffey, A. (2006) 'Multimodal ethnography', *Qualitative Research*, 6, 1, 77–96.

Dingwall, R. (1997) 'Accounts, interviews and observations', in Miller, G. and Dingwall, R. (eds.) *Context and Method in Qualitative Research*, London, Sage.

Douglas, J. (1976) *Investigative Social Research*, Beverley Hills CA, Sage.

Drew, P. (2006) 'When documents "speak": Documents, language and interaction', in Drew, P., Raymond, G., and Weinberg, D. (eds.) *Talk and Interaction in Social Research Methods*, London, Sage.

Duneier, M. (1992) *Slim's Table: Race, respectability, and masculinity*, Chicago, University of Chicago Press.

Duneier, M. (1999) *Sidewalk*, New York, Farrar, Straus and Giroux.

Duneier, M., (2002), 'What Kind of Combat Sport Is Sociology?', *American Journal of Sociology*, 107:6 (May 2002), 1551–1576.

Duneier, M. and Back, L. (2006) 'Voices from the sidewalk: Ethnography and writing race: Mitchell Duneier in conversation with Les Back (photos by Ovie Carter)', *Ethnic and Racial Studies*, 29, 3, 543–565.

Edwards, D. (1997) *Discourse and Cognition*, London, Sage.

Edwards, D. (2005) 'Discursive psychology', in K. L. Fitch and R. E. Sanders (eds.) *Handbook of Language and Social Interaction*, 257–273. Hillsdale NJ, Lawrence Erlbaum.

Edwards, D. and Potter, J. (1992) *Discursive Psychology*, London, Sage.

Eisner, E. (1992) 'Objectivity in educational research', *Curriculum Inquiry*, 22, 1, 9–15.

Ellis, C. (2004) *The Ethnographic I: a methodological novel about autoethnography*, Walnut Creek CA, Altamira.

Ellis, C. and Bochner, A. (eds.) (1996) *Composing Ethnography: Alternative Forms of Qualitative Writing*, Walnut Creek, CA, Altamira Press

Emmison, M. and Smith, P. (2000) *Researching the Visual*, London, Sage.

Erickson, F. (2011) 'A history of qualitative inquiry in social and educational research', in Denzin and Lincoln (eds.).

Fairclough, N. (2003) *Analysing Discourse: Textual Analysis for Social Research*, London, Routledge.

Faulkner, S. (2009) *Poetry as Method*, Walnut Creek CA, Left Coast Press.
Filstead, W. (ed.) (1970) *Qualitative Methodology*, Chicago, Markham.
Finch, J. (2007) 'Displaying families', *Sociology*, 41, 1, 65–81.
Finnegan, R. (1992) *Oral Traditions and the Verbal Arts: A guide to research practices*, London, Routledge.
Foucault, M. and Deleuze, G. (1977) 'Intellectuals and Power' in Foucault, M. *Language, Counter-Memory, Practice: Selected essays and interviews*, Edited by D. Bouchard, Ithaca NY, Cornell University Press (205–217).
Frake, C. (1964a) 'How to ask for a drink in Subanun', *American Anthropologist*, 66, 3, 127–132.
Frake, C. (1964b) 'A structural description of Subanun "religious behaviour"', in Goodenough, W. (ed.) *Explorations in Cultural Anthropology*, New York, McGraw Hill.
Gadamer, H-G (1984) 'The hermeneutics of suspicion', *Man and World*, 17, 3–4, 313–323.
Garfinkel, H. (1967) *Studies in Ethnomethodology*, Englewood Cliffs, NJ, Prentice-Hall.
Geertz, C. (1973) *The Interpretation of Cultures*, New York, Basic Books.
Geertz, C. (1988) *Works and Lives: the anthropologist as author*, Stanford CA, Stanford University Press.
Giorgi, A. and Giorgi, B. (2008) 'Phenomenology', in Smith (ed.).
Gobo, G. (2011) 'Back to Likert: Towards a conversational survey', in Williams and Vogt (eds.)
Goffman, E. (1959) *The Presentation of Self in Everyday Life*, Harmondsworth, Penguin.
Goffman, E. (1981) *Forms of Talk*, Philadelphia, University of Pennsylvania Press.
Gomm, R. (2001) 'Unblaming Victims and Creating Heroes: Reputational management in sociological writing', *Discourse: Studies in the Cultural Politics of Education*, 22, 2, 227–47.
Gouldner, A. (1973) *For Sociology: renewal and critique in sociology today*, Harmondsworth, Penguin.
Grahame, P. (1999) 'Doing qualitative research: three problematics', *Graduate Program in Applied Sociology*, 2, 1, 4–10, Boston University, Massachusetts.
Gubrium, J. and Holstein, J. (1990) *What is Family?*, Mountain View CA, Mayfield.

Gubrium, J. and Holstein, J. (1993) 'Phenomenology, Ethnomethodology, and Family Discourse', in Boss, P., Doherty, W., LaRossa, R., Schumm, W., and Steinmetz, S. (eds.) *Sourcebook of Family Theories and Methods: A Contextual Approach*, New York, Plenum.

Gubrium, J. and Holstein, J. (2001) Introduction, in Gubrium, J. and Holstein, J. (eds.) *Handbook of Interview Research*, Thousand Oaks CA, Sage.

Gutting, G. (1989) *Michel Foucault's Archaeology of Scientific Reason*, Cambridge, Cambridge University Press.

Haack, S. (2009) *Evidence and Inquiry: towards a reconstruction of epistemology*, Second edition, New York, Prometheus Press. (First edition published in 1993 by Blackwell.)

Halfpenny, P. (1982) *Positivism and Sociology*, London, Allen and Unwin.

Hammersley, M. (1989) *The Dilemma of Qualitative Method: Herbert Blumer and the Chicago Tradition*, London, Routledge.

Hammersley, M. (1992a) *What's Wrong with Ethnography?*, London, Routledge.

Hammersley, M. (1992b) 'The Paradigm Wars: Reports from the Front: Review of *The Paradigm Dialog* by E. Guba and *The Nature of Social and Educational Inquiry* by J. K. Smith', *British Journal of Sociology of Education*, 13, 1, 131–143.

Hammersley, M. (1994) 'Ethnographic writing', *Social Research Update* 5, Guildford, University of Surrey. Available at (accessed 24.11.11): http://sru.soc.surrey.ac.uk/SRU5.html

Hammersley, M. (1998) 'Partisanship and credibility: the case of anti-racist educational research', in P. Connolly and B. Troyna (eds) *Researching 'Race' in Educational Settings*, Buckingham, Open University Press.

Hammersley, M. (2000) *Taking Sides in Social Research*, London, Routledge.

Hammersley, M. (2003) '"Analytics" are No Substitute for Methodology: a response to Speer and Hutchby', *Sociology*, 37, 2, 339–51.

Hammersley, M. (2005) 'Ethnography and discourse analysis: incompatible or complementary?', *Polifonia*, 10, 1–20. Available at (accessed 11.12.11): http://cpd1.ufmt.br/meel/arquivos/artigos/3.pdf

Hammersley, M. (2008a) *Questioning Qualitative Inquiry*, London, Sage.

Hammersley, M. (2008b) 'Causality as conundrum: The case of qualitative inquiry' *Methodological Innovations Online*, 2, 3. Available at (accessed 7.1.12): http://erdt.plymouth.ac.uk/mionline/public_html/viewarticle.php?id=63&layout=html

Hammersley, M. (2009) 'Why Critical Realism Fails to Justify Critical Social Research', *Methodological Innovations Online* , 4, 2, 1–11.

Hammersley, M. (2011) *Methodology, Who Needs It?*, London, Sage.

Hammersley, M. (2012a) 'What's wrong with quantitative research?', in Cooper *et al.* (2012).

Hammersley, M. (2012b) 'Troubling theory in case study research', *Higher Education Research and Development*, 31, 3, 393–405.

Hammersley, M. and Atkinson, P. (2007) *Ethnography: Principles in practice*, Third edition, London, Routledge.

Hammersley, M. and Gomm, R. (2008) 'Assessing the radical critique of interviews', in Hammersley 2008a.

Hammersley, M. and Traianou, A. (2012) *Ethics in Qualitative Research*, London, Sage.

Hankinson, R. (1998) *The Sceptics*, Second edition, London, Routledge.

Harman, G. (2009). *Prince of Networks: Bruno Latour and Metaphysics*, Melbourne AU, re.press.

Harrington, A. (2000) 'In defence of verstehen and erklaren: Wilhelm Dilthey's ideas concerning a descriptive and analytical psychology', *Theory and Psychology*, 10, 4, 435–452.

Hartsock, N. (1987) 'The feminist standpoint: developing the ground for a specifically feminist historical materialism', in Harding, S. (ed.) *Feminism and Methodology: Social Science Issues*, Bloomington IND, Indiana University Press.

Hausheer, R. (1996) 'Three major originators of the concept of verstehen: Vico, Herder, Schleirmacher', *Philosophy*, 71, 278, 47–73.

Have, P. ten (2002) 'Ontology or methodology? Comments on Speer's "natural" and "contrived" data: a sustainable distinction?', *Discourse Studies*, 4, 527–30.

Have, P. ten (2004) *Understanding qualitative research and ethnomethodology*, London, Sage.

Have, P. ten (2007) *Doing Conversation Analysis: A Practical Guide*, Second edition, London, Sage.

Hegel, G. W. F. (1820) *Elements of the Philosophy of Right*, Cambridge, Cambridge University Press, 1991.

Heritage, J. (1984) *Garfinkel and Ethnomethodology*, Cambridge, Polity Press.

Hey, V. (1997) *The Company She Keeps: An ethnography of girls' friendships*, Buckingham, Open University Press.

Holliday, A. (2002) *Qualitative research*, London, Sage.

Hollway, W. (2005) 'Commentary 2', *Qualitative Studies in Psychology*, 2, 4, 312–4.

Howarth, D. (2000) *Discourse*, Buckingham, Open University Press, 2000.

Hutchinson, P., Read, R., and Sharrock, W. (2008) *There is No Such Thing as Social Science*, Aldershot, Ashgate.

James, I. (2012) *The New French Philosophy*, Cambridge, Polity.

Jay, M. (1996) *The Dialectical Imagination*, Berkeley, University of California Press. (First published in 1973.)

Jones, O. (2001) 'Before the dark of reason': some ethical and epistemological considerations on the otherness of childhood, *Ethics, Place and Environment*, 4, 2, 173–178.

Kaplan, I. (2008) 'Being "seen" being "heard": engaging with students on the margins of education through participatory photography', in Thomson, P. (ed.) *Doing Visual Research with Children and Young People*, London, Routledge.

Keat, R. and Urry, J. (1983) *Social Theory as Science*, Second edition, London, Routledge and Kegan Paul.

King, G., Keohane, R. O., and Verba, S. (1994) *Designing Social Inquiry*, Princeton, Princeton University Press.

Kolakowski, L (1972) *Positivist Philosophy*, Harmondsworth, Penguin.

Kuhn, T. (1970) *The Structure of Scientific Revolutions*, Second edition, Chicago, University of Chicago Press.

Law, J. (2004) *After Method: Mess in social science research*, London, Routledge.

Leach, E. (1957) 'The epistemological background to Malinowski's empiricism', in Firth, R. (ed.) *Man and Culture*, London, Routledge and Kegan Paul.

Leiter, B. (2005) 'The Hermeneutics of Suspicion: Recovering Marx, Nietzsche, and Freud', University of Texas Law, Public Law, Research Paper No. 72. Available at: http://ssrn.com/abstract=691002.

Levitas, R. (2005) *The Inclusive Society? Social Exclusion and the New Labour*, Second edition, Basingstoke, Palgrave Macmillan.

Lewis, J. (2006) 'Making Order out of a Contested Disorder: the utilisation of online support groups in social science research', *Qualitative Researcher*, Issue 3, 2006:4–7.

Lieberson, S. (1991) 'Small Ns and big conclusions: an examination of the reasoning based on a small number of cases', *Social Forces*, 70, 307–20.

Lieberson, S. (1994) 'More on the uneasy case for using Mill-type methods in small-N comparative studies', *Social Forces*, 72, 1225–37.

Lindesmith, A. (1937) *The Nature of Opiate Addiction*, Chicago, University of Chicago Libraries.

Lindesmith, A. (1968) *Addiction and Opiates*, Chicago, Aldine.

Loader I. and Sparks, R. (2010) 'Wacquant and civic sociology: "Formative intentions" and formative experiences', *Criminology and Criminal Justice*, 10, 4, 405–15.

Lundman, R. and McFarlane, P. (1976) 'Conflict methodology: an introduction and preliminary assessment', *Sociological Quarterly*, 17, 503–12.

Lynch, M. (1993) *Scientific Practice and Ordinary Action: Ethnomethodology and social studies of science*, Cambridge, Cambridge University Press.

Lynch, M. (2000) 'Against reflexivity as an academic virtue and source of privileged knowledge', *Theory, Culture and Society*, 17, 3, 26–54.

Macdonell, D. (1986) *Theories of Discourse: an introduction*, Oxford, Blackwell.

Macey, D. (1993) *The Lives of Michel Foucault*, NY, Pantheon.

MacLure, M. and Walker, B. (2000) 'Disenchanted Evenings: The social organization of talk in parent-teacher consultations' in UK secondary schools, *British Journal of Sociology of Education* 21, 1, 5–25

Mahoney, J. and Goertz, G. (2006) 'A tale of two cultures: contrasting quantitative and qualitative research', *Political Analysis*, 14, 227–49.

Malinowski, B. (1967) *A Diary in the Strict Sense of the Term*, London, Routledge and Kegan Paul.

Marlaire, C. and Maynard, D. (1990) 'Standardised testing as an interactional phenomenon', *Sociology of Education*, 63, 83–101.

Marsh, C. (1979) 'Problems with Surveys: Method or Epistemology?' *Sociology*, 13, 2, 293–305.

Matza, D. (1967) 'The disreputable poor', in Bendix, R. and Lipset, S. (eds.) *Class, Status and Power*, London, Routledge and Kegan Paul.

Matza, D. (1969) *Becoming Deviant*, Englewood Cliffs, Prentice Hall.

Maxwell J. (2012) *A Realist Approach to Qualitative Research*, Thousand Oaks CA, Sage.

May, R. Buford (2005) 'Shadowboxing: A Review of Loïc Wacquant's Body & Soul', *Symbolic Interaction*, 28, 429–431.

Meehl, P. (1954) *Clinical versus Statistical Prediction*, Minneapolis, University of Minnesota Press.

Merton, R. K., Sills, D, L., and Stigler, S. M. (1984) 'The Kelvin dictum and social science; an excursion into the history of an idea', *Journal of the History of the Behavioral Sciences*, 20, 319–31.

Miller, J. (1993) *The Passions of Michel Foucault*, New York, Simon and Schuster.

Mishler, E. (1991) *Research Interviewing: context and narrative*, Second edition, Cambridge MA, Harvard University Press.

Mishler, E. (2004) *Storylines: Craftartists' Narratives of Identity*, Second edition, Cambridge MA, Harvard University Press.

Mishler, E. (2005) 'Commentary 3', *Qualitative Research in Psychology*, 2, 4, 315–8.

Mitchell, R. (1991) 'Secrecy and disclosure in fieldwork', in Shaffir, W. and Stebbins, R. (eds.) *Experiencing fieldwork: An inside view of qualitative research*, Newbury Park CA, Sage.

Mitchell, R. (2001) *Dancing at Armageddon: survivalism and chaos in modern times*, Chicago, University of Chicago Press.

Moran, D. (2002) *Introduction to Phenomenology*, London, Routledge.

Morgan, D. (1996) *Family Connections: An introduction to family studies*, Cambridge, Polity Press.

Morgan, D. (2011a) 'Locating "Family Practices"', *Sociological Research Online*, 16 (4) 14. Available at (accessed 20.12.11): http://www.socresonline.org.uk/16/4/14.html

Morgan, D. (2011b) *Rethinking Family Practices*, Basingstoke, Palgrave Macmillan.

Morrow, R. with Brown, D. (1994) *Critical Theory and Methodology*, Thousand Oaks CA. Sage.

Morton, H. (1996) *Becoming Tongan: An ethnography of childhood*, Honolulu HI, University of Hawai'i Press.

Murphy, E., Dingwall, R., Greatbatch, D., Parker, S., and Watson, P. (1998) 'Qualitative research methods in health technology assessment: a review of the literature', *Health Technology Assessment*, 2(16), 1–260.

Available online (accessed 31 October 2011): http://www.hta.ac.uk/execsumm/summ216.htm

Murphy, E. and Dingwall, R. (2003) *Qualitative Methods and Health Policy Research*, New York, Aldine de Gruyter.

Newell, R. (1986) *Objectivity, Empiricism, and Truth*, London, Routledge and Kegan Paul.

Newman, K. (1999) *No Shame in My Game: the working poor in the inner city*, New York, Knopf.

Newman, K. (2002) 'No Shame: The View from the Left Bank', *American Journal of Sociology*, 107, 6, 1577–99.

Oakley, A. (2000) *Experiments in Knowing: Gender and method in the social sciences*, Cambridge, Polity Press.

Oliver, C. and O'Reilly, K. (2010) 'A Bourdieusian Analysis of Class and Migration: Habitus and the Individualizing Process', *Sociology* 44, 1, 49–66.

Olson, L., Wahab, S., Thompson, C., and Durrant, L. (2011) 'Suicide Notes Among Native Americans, Hispanics, and Anglos', *Qualitative Health Research*, 21, 11, 1484–1494.

Olson, R. (1993) *The Emergence of the Social Sciences 1642–1792*, New York, Twayne Press.

Outhwaite, W. (1976) *Understanding social life: The method called verstehen*, London, Allen and Unwin.

Palmer, R. (1969) *Hermeneutics*, Evanston ILL, Northwestern University Press.

Peräkylä, A. (1997) 'Validity and reliability in research based on tapes and transcripts', in Silverman, D. (ed) *Qualitative Analysis: Issues of Theory and Method*. London: Sage, 201–220. Revised edition 2003. Reprinted in Seale, C. (ed.) *Social Research Methods. A Reader*. London: Routledge (2003).

Pickering, M. (1993) *Auguste Comte: an intellectual biography*, three volumes, Cambridge, Cambridge University Press.

Pink, S. (2007) *Doing Visual Ethnography: Images, Media and Representation in Research*, Second edition, London, Sage.

Pink, S. (2009) *Doing Sensory Ethnography*, London, Sage.

Platt, J. (1996) *A History of Sociological Research Methods in America 1920–1960*, Cambridge, Cambridge University Press.

Plummer, K. (1983) *Documents of Life*, London, Unwin Hyman.

Plummer, K. (2001) *Documents of Life 2: An invitation to critical humanism*, Second edition, London, Sage.

Pollner, M. (1987) *Mundane Reason: Reality in everyday and sociological discourse*, Cambridge, Cambridge University Press.

Popper, K. (1957) *The Poverty of Historicism*, London, Routledge and Kegan Paul.

Potter, J. (1996) *Representing Reality: Discourse, rhetoric and social construction*, London, Sage.

Potter, J. (2002) 'Two kinds of natural', *Discourse Studies*, 4, 4, 539–42.

Potter, J. and Edwards, D. (2003) 'Rethinking Cognition: On Coulter on Discourse and Mind', *Human Studies* 26, 165–181.

Potter, J. and Wetherell, M. (1987) *Discourse and Social Psychology*, London, Sage.

Potter, J. and Hepburn, A. (2005a) 'Qualitative interviews in psychology: problems and possibilities', *Qualitative Research in Psychology*, 2, 4, 281–307

Potter, J. and Hepburn, A. (2005b) 'Authors' response', *Qualitative Research in Psychology*, 2, 4, 319–25.

Pound, P., Britten, N., Morgan, M., Yardley, L., Pope, C., Daker-White, G., and Campbell, R. (2005) 'Resisting medicines: a synthesis of qualitative studies on medicine taking', *Social Science and Medicine*, 61, 133–55.

Ragin, C. (2008) *Redesigning Social Inquiry*, Chicago, University of Chicago Press.

Rai, C. (2011) 'Positive loitering and public goods: The ambivalence of civic participation and community policing in the neoliberal city', *Ethnography*, 12, 1, 65–88.

Rainwater, L. and Pittman, D. (1967) 'Ethical problems in studying a politically sensitive and deviant community', *Social Problems*, 14, 357–66.

Rapley, T. (2001) 'The art(fulness) of open-ended interviewing: some considerations on analyzing interviews', *Qualitative Research*, 1, 3, 303–23.

Reason, P. and Bradbury, H. (eds.) (2001) *Handbook of Action research: participative inquiry and practice*, London, Sage.

Restivo, S. (2010) 'Bruno Latour: The once and future philosopher', in Ritzer, G. and Stepinsky, J. (eds.) *The New Blackwell Companion to Major Social Theorists*, Oxford, Blackwell. Available at (accessed 24.4.12): http://www.salrestivo.org/LatourFinal.10.pdf

Reinharz, S. (1997) 'Who am I? The need for a variety of selves in the field', in Hertz, R. (ed.) *Reflexivity and Voice*, London, Sage.

Richardson, L and St. Pierre, E. (2005) 'Writing: A Method of Inquiry', in Denzin, N. and Lincoln, Y. (eds.) *Handbook of Qualitative Research*, Third Edition, Thousand Oaks CA, Sage.

Riessman, C. (2008) *Narrative Analysis*, Second edition, London, Sage.

Rihoux, B. and Ragin, C. C. (2009) (eds.) *Configurational Comparative Methods: Qualitative Comparative Analysis (QCA) and Related Techniques*, London, Sage.

Roberts, C. (1996) *The Logic of Historical Explanation*, University Park PA, Pennsylvania State University Press.

Rose, G. (2007) *Visual Methodologies: An Introduction to the Interpretation of Visual Materials*, Second edition, London, Sage.

Sandelowski. M. (2004) 'Qualitative Research', in Lewis-Beck, M., Bryman, A., and Liao, T. (eds) *The Sage Encyclopedia of Social Science Research Methods*, Thousand Oaks CA, Sage.

Sanders, C. (2005) 'The Sweet (Social) Science', *Symbolic Interaction*, 28, 437–440.

Sayer, A. (2000) *Realism and Social Science*, London, Sage.

Scharff, R. (1995) *Comte after Positivism*, Cambridge, Cambridge University Press.

Schegloff, E. A. (1997) 'Whose text? Whose context?', *Discourse and Society*, 8, 2, 165–87.

Schrodt, P. (2006) 'Beyond the linear frequentist orthodoxy', *Political Analysis*, 14, 3, 335–339.

Schutz, A. (1962) *Collected Paper Volumes 1–3*, The Hague, Martinus Nijhoff.

Schwandt, T. (2001) *Dictionary of Qualitative Inquiry*, Second edition, Thousand Oaks CA, Sage.

Seierstad, A. (2004) *The Bookseller of Kabul*, London, Virago.

Shapin, S. (1994) *A Social History of Truth*, Chicago, University of Chicago Press.

Sharrock, W. and Read, R. (2002) *Kuhn: philosopher of scientific revolution*, Cambridge, Cambridge University Press.

Sieber, S. D. (1973) 'The integration of fieldwork and survey methods', *American Journal of Sociology*, 78, 6, 1335–1359.

Sigmund, P. (1971) *Natural Law in Political Thought*, Cambridge MS, Winthrop.

Silverman, D. (1997) 'Towards an aesthetics of research', in D. Silverman (ed.) *Qualitative Research: theory, method and practice*, London, Sage.

Silverman, D. (2006) *Interpreting Qualitative Data*, Third edition, London, Sage.

Silverman, D. (2007) *A Very Short, Fairly Interesting, and Reasonably Cheap Book About Qualitative Research*, London, Sage.

Smith, J. (ed.) (2008) *Qualitative Psychology: A practical guide to research methods*, Second edition, London, Sage.

Smith, J. (2005) 'Commentary 1', *Qualitative Research in Psychology*, 2, 4, 309–11.

Smith, J., Flowers, P., and Larkin, M. (2009) *Interpretative Phenomenological Analysis*, London, Sage.

Smith, J. and Osborn, M. (2008) 'Interpretative phenomenological analysis', in Smith (ed.).

Speer, S. (2002) '"Natural" and "contrived" data: a sustainable distinction?', *Discourse Studies*, 4, 4, 511–25.

Speer, S. A. and Hutchby, I. (2003a) 'From ethics to analytics: aspects of participants' orientations to the presence and relevance of recording devices', *Sociology*, 37, 2, 315–37.

Speer, S. A. and Hutchby, I. (2003b) 'Methodology Needs Analytics: A Rejoinder to Martyn Hammersley', *Sociology*, 37, 2, 353–359.

Stouffer, S. (1930) An Experimental Comparison of Statistical and Case-History Methods in Attitude Research, PhD thesis, University of Chicago. Reprinted: New York, Arno Press, 1980.

Styles, J. (1979) 'Researching Gay Baths', *Urban Life* , 8, 2, 135–52.

Tapper, N. (2006) *Bartered Brides: politics, gender and marriage in an Afghan tribal society*, Cambridge, Cambridge University Press.

Tashakkori, A. and Teddlie, C. (eds.) (2010) *Handbook of Mixed Methods in Social and Behavioral Research*, Second edition, Thousand Oaks CA, Sage.

Taylor, C. (1985) *Philosophy and the Human Sciences: Philosophical papers 2*, Cambridge, Cambridge University Press.

Taylor, S. (2012) *What is Discourse Analysis?*, London, Bloomsbury.

Taylor, S. and Littleton, K. (2006) 'Biographies in talk: A narrative-discursive research approach', *Qualitative Sociology Review*, 1, 2. Available at (accessed 7.1.12): http://www.qualitativesociologyreview.org/ENG/Volume3/QSR_2_1_Taylor_Littleton.pdf

Thomson, R., Kehily, M.J., Hadfield, L. and Sharpe, S. (2011) *Making Modern Mothers*, Bristol, Policy Press.

Thomson, Sir William (Lord Kelvin) (1889) *Popular Lectures and Addresses*, volume 1, London, Macmillan.

Trow, M. (1957) 'Comment on participant observation and interviewing: A comparison', *Human Organization*, 16, 33–35.

Truzzi, M. (ed.) (1974) *Verstehen: Subjective understanding in the social sciences*, Reading MS, Addison-Wesley.

Tyler, S. (ed.) (1969) *Cognitive Anthropology*, New York, Holt, Rinehart and Winston.

Tyler, S. (1992) 'On being out of words', in Marcus, G. (ed.) *Rereading Cultural Anthropology*, Durham NC, Duke University Press.

Van Dijk, T. (1991) *Racism and the Press*, London, Routledge.

Venkatesh, S. (2008) *Gang Leader for a Day*, London, Allen Lane.

Vogt, K. (2010) 'Ancient skepticism', in *Stanford Encyclopedia of Philosophy*. Available at (accessed 9.1.12): http://plato.stanford.edu/entries/skepticism-ancient/

Wacquant, L. (1997) 'Three pernicious premises in the study of the American ghetto', *International Journal of Urban and Regional Research*, 21, 2, 341–53.

Wacquant, L. (2002) 'Scrutinizing the Street: Poverty, Morality, and the Pitfalls of Urban Ethnography', *American Journal of Sociology*, 107, 6, 1468–1532.

Wacquant, L. (2004) *Body and Soul: Notebooks of an Apprentice Boxer*, New York: Oxford University Press.

Wacquant, L. (2005) 'Shadowboxing with Ethnographic Ghosts: A Rejoinder', *Symbolic Interaction*, 28, 3, 441–447.

Wacquant, L. (2008) *Urban Outcasts: A comparative sociology of advanced marginality*, Cambridge, Polity Press.

Wacquant, L. (2009) *Prisons of Poverty*. Minneapolis, MN, University of Minnesota Press.

Wacquant, L. and Wilson, W. (1993) 'The cost of racial and class exclusion in the inner city', in Wilson (ed.).

Wax, M. (1972) 'Tenting with Malinowski', *American Sociological Review*, 37, 1, 1–13.

Wetherell, M. and Edley, N. (1999) 'Negotiating Hegemonic Masculinity: Imaginary Positions and Psycho-Discursive Practices', *Feminism and Psychology*, 9, 3, 335–356.

Wetherell, M., Taylor, S. and Yates, S. (eds) (2001) *Discourse theory and practice*, London: Sage.

Wieder, D. (1974) *Language and Social Reality*, The Hague, Mouton.

Williams, M. and Vogt, W. P. (eds.) (2011) *The Sage Handbook of Innovation in Social Research Methods*, London, Sage.

Wilson, W. (1993a) 'The underclass: issues, perspectives, and public policy', in Wilson (ed.).

Wilson, W. (ed.) (1993b) *The Ghetto Underclass: Social Science Perspectives*, Newbury Park CA, Sage.

Wilson, W. (2009) *More Than Just Race: Being Black and Poor in the Inner City*, New York, W. W. Norton.

Wilson, W. and Chaddha, A. (2009) The role of theory in ethnographic research', *Ethnography*,10, 2–3, 269–284.

Wood, A. (1981) *Karl Marx*, London, Routledge and Kegan Paul.

Wright, R. and Decker, S. (1997) *Armed Robbers in Action*, Lebanon NH, Northeastern University Press.

Wright, T. (1986) *The Religion of Humanity: The impact of Comtean positivism on Victorian England*, Cambridge, Cambridge University Press.

Znaniecki, F. (1934) *The Method of Sociology*, New York, Farrar and Rinehart.

Index

NAME INDEX

SUBJECT INDEX